Edward Stuart Talbot

Slavery as Affected by Christianity

Edward Stuart Talbot

Slavery as Affected by Christianity

ISBN/EAN: 9783744734509

Printed in Europe, USA, Canada, Australia, Japan

Cover: Foto ©ninafisch / pixelio.de

More available books at **www.hansebooks.com**

SLAVERY AS AFFECTED BY CHRISTIANITY.

———

" Christianity never began by external alterations: for these, wherever they did not begin from the inward man and fix there their first and firm foundation, would always have failed in their salutary designs." NEANDER.

CONTENTS.

CHRISTIANITY made its appearance in the world, believers and rationalists would agree, at a congenial epoch. Speculation seemed vaguely to have acknowledged, or to be feeling after, truths to which Christianity alone gave a definite and coherent expression: the political circumstances of the time—its destructive as well as its constructive forces—the annihilation of local distinctions and the wider intercourse of the nations seemed to be favourable to the recognition of the new ideas, to assist their dissemination, and to enable them to produce more practical effects. To this all have agreed, because all have an interest in the proof. The believer sees evidence of the care with which an all-wise Providence made straight the path for the new revelation: while from the same facts the sceptic claims to gain a justification for his inference that Christianity is in no distinctive sense supernatural, but merely the natural outgrowth and inevitable climax of antecedent and contemporary tendencies. Hence it appears from the evidence of both sides, that had Christianity never appeared, there were forces at work which would have produced results not wholly dissimilar to those which she achieved. These forces were not annihilated by Christianity. They worked on side by side with her, sometimes independently, sometimes showing their own influence by assisting and securing acceptance for her. Thus the first difficulty in a subject like the present, is to discover how much is to be allotted after all fair deductions to the action of Christianity.

B

It may be added, that this difficulty is not peculiar to the period at which Christianity first appeared. In later times, the middle ages for instance, though she was in the field from the beginning, yet other forces came into existence beside her, such as those which social or economical changes generated, which cannot be called in any sense Christian, and whose action must be discriminated from that of Christianity[a].

In both cases the difficulty remains: and it is enhanced in proportion as we recognize the similarity of principle and plan between God's ordinary and natural, and His extraordinary and supernatural dealings with mankind: a similarity which in part results from the employment of human instruments, but which, whatever its cause, implies the liability in its degree of God's revealed religion to the same vicissitudes and conditions—those for instance of slow progress, of alternating success and defect, and of degeneracy and perversion, which beset the history of uninspired systems. It works to outward appearances as other influences work; hence the increased difficulty of separating its achievements from theirs.

The recognition of this truth, which perhaps we owe in part to the better side of the thought of the present day, will help to remove a second difficulty which occurs in an inquiry like the present. It may be called a difficulty of language. What in the history of Christianity is to be called failure? What success? But obviously it is much more than a mere verbal question. The reason why one person will congratulate himself on the success of Christianity where another is mourning its failure, lies in the fact that the two have formed completely different ideals as to

[a] So true is this, that a late writer (Rev. W. Church, Sermons) thinks that he discerns such a movement of society and opinion parallel with the movement set going by Christianity, and tending towards *some* of its results, yet distinguishable from it, and dependent upon different forces.

the extent in which Christianity may be expected to triumph. Is she to conquer all evil and reign? or is this her future and not her present destiny, while here she must be content to wage a ceaseless battle against predominating forces of evil, and be satisfied to hold a small part of the field of battle as her own? Were this question resolved, it would be easy to deal with a special point, like that of slavery. The particular case would probably correspond to the general rule; and an *à priori* opinion would act as interpreter to the evidence of history. As it is, it is necessary to begin at the other end. The solution of the particular case may throw light upon the larger and more difficult problem; and knowing what Christianity has done against slavery, it will be easier to judge what has been, or is likely to be, her success in the wider issues of her general struggle against the manifold evil of the world.

There is no reason why we should not anticipate so far as to say, that the history of slavery countenances the less sanguine view, since briefly that history appears to be as follows. In the first great contest, when Christianity encountered the slave-institutions of the Roman Empire, it failed to destroy them; for they never were destroyed until Roman society was attacked and inundated from the North. In the second struggle, waged against the villeinage of the middle ages, villeinage was indeed abolished: but it resisted for eight centuries, and only disappeared when other causes adequate to its destruction had come into existence. The history of the third, in which the absolute slavery inflicted on the negro and other "inferior" races is the opponent, remains unfinished: it is the part of the story on which Christianity looks with most pride, for abolition where it has been accomplished, was the result of definite measures, whose supporters have acted on christian motives. Yet abolition had been delayed for three Christian centuries: it was carried through at a crisis for other reasons favourable: it would probably never have taken place, but for the peculiar political position of the communities in question, which enabled a distant government, not directly influenced by colonial interests, to force it upon them.

Thus, if the question of abolition be taken as a test, there is surely reason to abstain from rhetorical declamation and too enthusiastic fancies as to the triumphs of Christianity. Such exaggeration is not only dangerous but unnecessary. Christianity has its triumphs, but they are quiet and gradual; it cannot conquer the world: but it incessantly maintains the attack; it achieves many a victory of detail; it often asserts its conquering power in the midst of defeat. Turn from the question of abolition to consider how Christianity has, at different times, mitigated, alleviated, and removed many of the harsher and more degrading features of slavery, and her power and her fidelity to her Divine mission become alike apparent. In this connexion two points are specially noticeable. First, that upon slavery at large her influence was more generally effective in the second, or mediæval, struggle, when her power dominated, in some sense, the whole of society, than in the first, when she had not acquired her most extensive dominion; or in the third, when she has been feebly represented in the slave countries, and when a part of society has again escaped from her restraints. Secondly, that her attacks on the worst features of these institutions were conducted by an appeal to principles which were really hostile to the whole system; and thus public opinion was gradually trained to welcome abolition, when in due time other causes made it ready. And, since a strong opinion may resist any change, however much all else may demand it, Christianity did in this manner no small service even to the cause of abolition.

It may be well to add, parenthetically, that throughout this Essay it is assumed that slavery is, in the abstract,

inconsistent with the whole spirit of Christianity; but that
it is not inferred that Christianity would attempt its abolition at all times and places. This is extremely important,
because it follows that Christianity is not always to be
accused of failure, when slavery is seen to remain. It is
impossible to fail, where there is no attempt. The proviso
is the more necessary, because it is difficult to avoid em-
ploying the language of failure.

It seems then that an account of the mitigating influences
of Christianity should occupy the greater part of an essay
on the present subject, while its contributions to the cause
of abolition will naturally come in for notice by implication
and incidentally.

Such an account falls naturally into two parts, (I) an
à priori treatment of the subject, containing an examination
of the principles of Christianity, the objects at which it
aimed, and the powers which it wielded in reference to
slavery, so far as these are common to all times and places;
(II) an à posteriori treatment, which will include the special
circumstances which at different times increased or di-
minished the forces of the Church, as well as the use which
she made of her weapons, the extent of her successes, and
the reasons of her failures. This second part, being
historical, must be divided according to the three great
periods already alluded to: (i) The period of the Empire;
(ii) the Middle Ages; (iii) the era of Modern or Negro
Slavery.

I. The key to the relations which Christianity in the abstract
bears to slavery is to be found in the fact, almost surprising
but quite characteristic, that it contains no positive or direct
prohibition of slavery by Christ or His Apostles. Christians
of different centuries have pledged themselves to a declaration of the absolute sinfulness of the institution at certain
times and in certain places—their own age, or their own
country. They have done so, and have been justified in

doing so. For though Christianity is identified with no political system, it must be possible that a political institution should reach a point of degeneracy and evil which the Church, as guardian of Christian interests in its own generation, can not look upon in silence. But the Founder of Christianity, and his immediate followers, were in a different position. They spoke to their own age, but they spoke also to all times and to every nation of the future. They had to lay everlasting foundations. They were inaugurating a religion which was to be fit for every condition in which human nature might be found. To admit any directly political matter into their teaching, would have been equivalent to limiting its possible sphere. Political philosophers tell us, that to certain nations slavery may be necessary; and it is certain that in other cases states (of which Rome may have been, and probably was, one) may have come to a condition in which the sudden destruction of their slave-institutions would be the destruction of society. Had Christianity lain under the obligation which the registration in her original documents of a positive prohibition against slavery would have involved, she must have constantly inaugurated revolutions, which would have always cost her opportunities of work for more important objects; and would sometimes have been actually pernicious, either impossible in the existing state of things, or premature, or sudden at a crisis when the general good demanded that they should be gradual. She would have irrevocably alienated one part of society; she would have led the other part to fix their eyes on political objects, while they would have postponed any attention to her spiritual teaching. The anarchy of a slave insurrection is not the most promising field for the Christian missionary. This would have been her history, if she had lived to see it. But at the outset she would have had to give battle to the institutions of the Roman Empire, and (with reverence be it said—with reverence it may be said, since the hypothetical case does not represent the course which God's providence had marked out for her—) she must have perished in the encounter.

How different was the method actually adopted at the foundation of Christianity, the precepts of the New Testament, which regulate the conduct of the slave and of the master, are enough to show. As regards the system, there is not a word of approbation, or of condemnation; it is assumed to exist, and individuals are shown how to comport themselves under it. In the Apostolical Constitutions a revolutionary reputation is deprecated[b]. Similarly, when the Church became dominant, the laws as to the ordination of slaves are her witnesses, that she gave no encouragement to anarchical or revolutionary attempts. Rather than do so, she went so far as to retract the spiritual gift once given. The slave ordained without his master's consent was to be unfrocked. These laws occur early, and they come not merely from Christian Emperors[c], but from Popes[d] and Ecclesiastics.

The canons of the Council of Gangra in Paphlagonia, held about the middle of the fourth century, against the Eustathians, a local sect of mystical and ascetic opinions, exhibits the orthodox Church contending against the anarchical teaching of the heretics. The Eustathians set great value on prayer, and would have had men desert their duties to spend their time in praying. The Council lays an anathema upon all who in this way, " prætextu divini cultûs," desert their masters. In this way Christianity behaved to slavery as she has behaved to all other established institutions. It was the boast of the apologists

[b] Διδάσκεσθω εὐχαριστεῖν τῷ δεσπότῃ, ἵνα μὴ βλασφημῆται ὁ λόγος. Lib. viii. c. 32.

[c] Valentinian, iii. Novell. 12.

[d] S. Leo. Ep. i. cap 1 Can. Apost. in Nov 123, . 17

that the Christians were in all respects faithful subjects of the laws.

But not only did Christianity not forbid slavery, she had few specific rules about the treatment of slaves. Hence it might seem that her influence was similar to that of the philosophical schools, theoretical in the main, and only incidentally practical. This would be a misleading comparison; but to dwell for a moment upon the action of philosophy upon slavery will illustrate, in more than one way, the distinctive characteristics of that of Christianity. Roman philosophy alone needs to be considered. Usually philosophy has but a remote bearing upon practice, because its doctrines are abstract, and its pupils men of speculation rather than of action. In both respects the school of Roman Stoicism differed from its Greek predecessors. Exhausted by the variety and ill-success of previous speculative attempts, driven in upon themselves by the jealousy of a despotism which closed the avenues of a political career, and stimulated by the revolting corruption of the times to seek more earnestly for an antidote, men looked for a spiritual director rather than an ingenious thinker; they preferred precept to theory, practical advice to soaring speculation. Philosophy, deferring to their altered mood, ceased to be metaphysical and transcendental, and became moral. The change brought to her knees a new class of pupils, and an enlarged sphere of influence.

Among the Stoics were practical men, a large section of the Roman bar, statesmen, like Cicero—great nobles, who, if ignorant themselves, at least conformed to the fashion and kept a philosopher;—and, in the case of Marcus Aurelius, even the emperor himself. To these men, philosophy, no longer the speculative pastime of a few, but the guide and director of practical life, spoke in the practical language of moral precept. Thus it was an exceptional moment. In earlier times slavery had had to deal with less practical forms of philosophy, and had defied them, or won their support. In modern Europe philosophy, if political economy be excepted, has hardly exercised, if it now exercises, any influence apart from Christianity.

The claim of Stoicism, therefore, to be regarded as one of the forces which anticipated the action of Christianity, and acted " in unconscious alliance" with it, depends upon the character of the moral ideas for which, in its didactic phase, it secured practical influence. These moral ideas drew their life from two master-beliefs:

α. The belief in the dignity and self-dependence of human nature.

β. The belief in the equality of mankind as citizens of the world.

The last has been often dwelt upon. It was the reflection upon thought of external events, of the extension of Roman citizenship completed by Caracalla, and the destruction by Macedonian and Roman conquests of the barriers between nations. The notion of universal equality was opposed to all the most cherished ideas of the ancient world, their municipal, local, and corporate traditions; and, therefore, although it followed logically from the appeal to Nature (φύσις) which the Stoics made, it was only established in public opinion when circumstances enabled it to appear as the mere expansion of an earlier notion. Rome made it easy for people to grasp the conception of the world, as a reality to which all belonged, by making her own Empire and her own citizenship world-embracing. This notion thus introduced became the central truth of all thought and belief under the Empire: or, rather, all thought caught from it its form and colour. Hence its importance is not that which attaches to the assertion of a single truth, however significant. It is that of a spirit pervading all literature and opinion, which gives a clue to the temper and tendencies of the day. The theory constantly recurring in the pages of the heathen writers passed into christian thought to culminate in Augustine's City of God.

Taken by itself, it shattered the old defences of slavery. Beside it, the theories of inferior races, of "the natural ruler," and the "natural servant" disappeared; its influence is to be seen in the change of position adopted by those who were still obliged to defend slavery as a political institution, namely, the lawyers. Slavery is contrary to the law of nature, said Ulpian; and his school were obliged to apologize for it as the result of conquest—a barbarous theory, because it condemned to slavery, according to the caprice of fortune, those whom nature least intended for it: but perhaps, on that very account, ready more easily in its turn to collapse. Slavery is contrary to the law of nature, repeats Justinian; and when he proceeds to derive it from the law of nations, people must have been struck by the disparity in a single instance of two codes otherwise perfectly harmonious, and must have drawn the obvious moral.

Such were the effects of the theory by itself. The philosophers gave it new influence, when they drew from it an inference of moral obligation. This either took the religious form: according to which, all alike were children of one celestial father, a Jupiter, whom none knew, yet in whom many tried vainly to believe; and, in virtue of this common tie, owed duties, heaven-imposed, to one another: or it appeared in a strictly moral shape, according to modern language, as a Philosophy of Benevolence. Men were taught that they were equals, and bidden to treat each other with the courtesy and respect due to equals. They were taught that they were fellow-citizens of the commonwealth of the world, and therefore owed duties and mutual assistance to one another.

The last-mentioned theory lowered the individual. It set all men on an equal level; each man might seem lost

among the many. But such a tendency was counteracted
by the other great doctrine of the Stoics, which asserted the
need of self-dependence and self-respect. Artificial distinctions were nothing; the real distinction was that which
a man conferred upon himself—the difference between the
wise and foolish, between the good and the uncontrolled or
evil. This bore at once upon the case of the slave, for in a
country to which Greek slaves had, in great measure,
brought learning and philosophy—where these very doctrines were being taught by the slave, Epictetus—could
any one doubt that this true inward dignity might be a
slave's possession? Could it be right that accident should
subject such an one to the capricious cruelty of a master?
The attack upon existing institutions was symbolized by
the rejection of ordinary language. Slavery so-called, says
Seneca over and over again, the slavery of the body, is not
slavery at all; there is but one true slavery—the thraldom
of the soul to passion and evil. This doctrine had a double
effect. The master felt that he had no moral superiority
over his slave, and that if he retained his legal rights over
him, they must be exercised in the most moderate way.
The slave was taught to care less for the outward slavery,
which was merely nominal: he fell back in magnanimous
confidence upon his inward liberty. Such, at least, was
Seneca's frequent exhortation, if the voice of Seneca ever
reached him.

These are the doctrines of Stoicism: noble and humane,
bearing, as we cannot doubt and can partly trace, practical
fruits. But there are two objections to a system based on
self-respect. First, it does not draw out sympathies; a
man relies on himself; as to others, he would be inde-
pendent of them. Pity was a weakness with the Stoics:
pride is not akin to tenderness, and self-reliance easily
becomes spiritual pride. Secondly, such a system brings
to bear upon a man only one class of motives; the external

motives are forgotten : to the influence of an inward ideal everything is entrusted.

After these two criticisms, to which others will be added incidentally in the sequel, this survey of Stoic teaching may be used to bring out Christian methods by comparison and contrast. Now the gist of the difference between the two lies in this, that Christianity did not so much teach men new doctrines, as put them into a new position. Stoicism had faintly anticipated this characteristic, when it awoke men to the consciousness of their position as citizens of the commonwealth of the world: yet this was not a new position, nor was it expressed by anything new in outward facts. But Christianity proclaimed that with the Incarnation ' all things had become new ;' and in regard to men the great novelty lay in the Membership of Christ. This great doctrine underlies probably more of the New Testament than is commonly supposed. The true vine, the body which hath many members[e], are the metaphorical expression given to it by Christ and His Apostle. Not only did Christ die for men: it was by becoming part of Him that they obtained the benefits of His redemption. Through this men are brought into unspeakable nearness to God[f]. They seem almost to lose their individuality, in order to live again with a life that was Christ's life[g]. From this, as from the great first premise[h], St. Paul seems to deduce all the duties of Christians to one another, the destruction of all arbitrary distinctions between men, among them of this very one between freemen and slaves[i]. The passages, which by themselves seem merely to speak of unity, imply, if their phraseology is examined, nothing less than this unity in membership. Moreover, this doctrine gave a new expression, and a deeper meaning, to old beliefs.

[e] 1 Cor. xii. 12. et passim in S. Paul.
[f] Col. iii. 3. [g] Gal. ii. 20.
[h] Col. iii. 10. (cf. Gal. iii. 27.) and perhaps 17. [i] Gal. iii. 28.

As members of Christ, men were made more truly children of God[k]. By conformity to His image[l], by being changed into His likeness, they revived the traces, never wholly obliterated, of the primal likeness between God and man[m]. Even the bond of common humanity was drawn closer when they became one in the new man, " putting on Christ Jesus." Lastly, the members of that Being, in whom dwelt all the fulness of the Godhead, were, as well their bodies[n] as their spirits, temples of the Holy Spirit, and of the Blessed Trinity : each soul a temple by itself, or, in a changed figure, each soul forming one stone in the great Temple, whose corner-stone is Christ[o]. Thus both the doctrine itself, and each of its consequence, gave to each Christian soul an infinitely valuable and sacred cha- racter : the privileges drew men to God; the common participation in them drew men to one another.

But Christianity did more than tell men of their new position ; she placed them in it, and impressed it upon their senses as well as upon their reason. By an outward rite she admitted them to her privileges, and while this produced the closest possible tie between those who were baptized[p], it did not beget exclusiveness towards those without, because Christianity taught that all men, even heathens, were already in part, and might at any time become by baptism completely, possessed of the benefits of redemption and the rights of membership[q]. Thus admitted, the mem- bers of the Christian society were reminded of their unity among themselves, and equality before God, by a common worship. For this, Christ Himself had instituted a rite, which renewed, while it expressed with solemn and startling vivid- ness, that union of men which flowed from a common partici- pation in His own nature. The circumstances with which

[k] Rom. viii. 15, with the whole context. [l] Rom. viii. 29.
[m] Gen. i. 26. Col. iii. 10. [n] 1 Cor. vi. 19; iii. 16.
[o] Eph. ii. 20—22. [p] 1 Cor. xii. 13.
[q] cf. Aug. in Ps. xxv. 2. sect. 2.

the early Church surrounded this feast, the Agapè and the kiss of peace, only developed the intrinsic character of the Divine ordinance itself. Yet, so close was this intimacy, that the heathen could not give to it anything but a sensual meaning; and that in later times actual corruptions, which too nearly justified these suspicions, made the abolition of the ceremonies necessary. One distinction, and one only, was known in the Church, the distinction of spiritual gifts; whether, as in early times, resulting from direct and anomalous inspiration, or from the ordinary endowments of the Ministry. To these distinctions, slave and freeman, high and low, were alike eligible. Even in her worldly days, and in times when everywhere else class distinctions had taken a caste-like rigidity, the Church did not altogether, though she did almost, desert her noble principles of equality in this respect. In the ninth century a high ecclesiastic[q] still complains of the detestable practice, "ut ex vilissimis servis fiant summi pontifices;" and, in the twelfth, the proudest of the Hohenstauffen is obliged to hold the stirrup of the poor scholar of St. Albans.

Thus to the Christian his relation to his fellow members was constantly brought home by the associations amidst which he lived: the citizenship of the City of God upon earth was something far more palpable than the Stoic's citizenship of the world; just as the membership of Christ was a living reality, to which there is no parallel among the Stoics, but a faint surmise[r].

But he was not left to the influence which his realization of the doctrines of the Faith and of their bearing upon life might exercise upon his conscience. He was worked upon by example and precept. His Lord Himself had, we may be sure, followed the manual labour which the freemen of

[q] Thegan, biographer of Louis le Debonnaire. Cit. ap. Milman, Lat. Christ. ii. 330.

[r] v. Denis Idées Morales dans Antiquité, ii. 169.

the empire thought fit only for slaves: His Apostle was not afraid to say that He had taken upon Him the form of a slave (μορφὴν δούλου)[s]: He died by a slave's death, and His disciples were drawn from the class to which He had condescended to belong. Like Him the Apostle of the Gentiles laboured with his hands, and men of low class and slaves became preachers of the Gospel. So much for the examples which rescued slavery from its contempt. In the way of direct teaching the Apostles did not allow the general exhortations to love and mercy toward others, which cover the pages of inspired Scripture, to remain without specific application to the case of slavery. They taught slave and master alike to raise their eyes to heaven, and to treat slavery according to the revelations of Faith. The master learnt his responsibility to God for any cruelty to one of God's children[t]: the slave saw that by diligent service he was serving God, and not man, and that in due time his reward would be given to him[u]. Both alike knew that (in a phrase which obtained a significant degree of currency in the Apostolic Church) with God there was no " acceptance of persons[x]." These precepts too come, as is usual with S. Paul, close upon the statement of the great doctrines which give them force[y]. Upon the differences between true and false slavery S. Paul, like Seneca, frequently assists in language borrowed from the schools. The bondage to sin[z], and similarly bondage under the law[a], is contrasted on one side with the outward slavery which to Christ's freeman is as nothing; and, on the other, with the bondage to Christ, which is itself perfect freedom[b]. But the inspired writer avoided the paradoxes

---

[s] Phil. ii. 7.   [t] Col. iv. 1. Eph. vi. 9.

[u] Col. iii. 22, 24. Eph. vi. 5—8.

[x] S. Paul, Col. iii. 25. S. Peter, Acts x. 34. S. James, ii. 1.

[y] See, for instance, the connection between Col. iii. 22. and vv. 10, 11. of the same chapter.

[z] Rom. vi. 17.   [a] Gal. iv. 3.   [b] 1 Cor. vii. 21.

of the Stoic. He does not say that it matters nothing to a
man whether he is a slave or free, for he bids Christian
freemen not to become slaves, and Christian slaves to seize
any opportunity of escaping from slavery. Such at least
is the interpretation usually set upon the words " use it
rather," (μᾶλλον χρῆσαι.) But the support given to the other
rendering, " prefer thy present position", by such men as
Chrysostom, Theodoret, &c., shows how completely they
recognized the triumph of Christianity over the opprobrium
of slavery. Finally, the trade of the slave dealer is condemned in a catalogue of heinous crimes.

It is impossible at this point to omit all notice of a doctrine
which, though it cannot be said to have any direct authority
from inspiration, was through a great part of Church history
so generally accepted[c], that it acquired some of the influence
of the more certain and genuine parts of Christian teaching—
the doctrine that slavery was the effect of sin. The principle
was remarkable for its many-sidedness. Christ has redeemed
us from sin, and so has cancelled the best title deeds of
the slave-holder. Since all are sinners, the master cannot
oppress the slave who bears the burthens of a sin of which
he was not alone guilty: the slave was not a sinner above all
the Galilæans. The slave must bear patiently a yoke which
his sins have deserved. Here were three different inferences:
it was possible to draw one of rather a different kind, and
extract from the principle a justification for the continuance
of slavery among Christians[d]. But a slave system which
consciously adopted this defence, could not be other than
humane.

Two points remain to be observed. First, that Christianity, unlike the philosophies, undertook to supply supernatural assistance for the discharge of charity, as of other

[c] It is taught by Aug. and Chrys. It reappears in a Canon of Aachen, 816,
Hard. iv. 1115, as an accepted truth.

[d] C. of Aachen, sup.

virtues. She taught that such grace was necessary for holiness: and thus, while Stoicism inculcated a self-reliance, which, as has been seen, was apt to harden the heart, Christianity doubly abased the man whom it was to exalt, by showing him that, without the original gift of redemption, no effort of his own could restore him, and that even as it is, those efforts could not be made, except by a strength which was not his own. Lowly, and therefore tender,—forgiving, because forgiven. This is one of the most attractive aspects of the christian character, and one in which other beliefs have been least able to imitate it. Secondly, and lastly, it is to be observed that the Christian was not left to his own conscience, but was roused by a sense of responsibility to a God, in whose hands lay infinite issues of reward and punishment.

The evidence which has now been adduced, is sufficient to supply, so to speak, a solution à priori to the present question. There can be no doubt how a religion founded on such principles, and teaching such doctrines would " affect slavery." Its influence would be of a twofold character. So it often happens when a new doctrine takes hold of men's minds. They see at once its most patent consequences: they remedy those details of their conduct, or of things about them, which are glaringly inconsistent with their new principles. This comes quickly. But slowly, after a long interval, as the principles work more deeply into their mind, as they use and dwell upon them for the purpose of their first contest, they perceive that the changes which they really demand are far more comprehensive: that nothing less than an entire reconstruction will be sufficient: that things hitherto unquestioned, and assumed as natural, universal, and necessary facts, must give way. This is the second harvest of results; it comes later, but it is often the wealthiest of the two. So it was when Christianity met slavery. The selfishness, cruelty, and corruption, which were the abuses of the institution, were at once attacked: they could be maintained by no one who called himself a Christian. But without slavery in some form men could not conceive of society: it would not have occurred to any one to question it. It was only as the fight went on that Christians learnt that the arguments which they advanced against the abuses of slavery were radically inconsistent with its existence. Thus Christianity had its two harvests,—the first, while it was engaged in ameliorating the abuses of slavery; the second, when the conviction matured itself that slavery itself was unchristian.

II. From this enquiry, which indicates how Christianity *ought to* affect slavery, it is necessary to turn to history and seek there a solution *à posteriori;* to enquire how far Christianity has obtained its two harvests; to what purpose, and under what special circumstances of advantage or disadvantage, it has wielded its weapons: in a word, looking backwards to decide how it *has* affected slavery.

And thus (i) in the Roman Empire, (ii) in the new nations of the Middle Ages, (iii) in modern times.

(i) In tracing the effects of Christianity upon Roman slavery, we look first to the law. This had been for some time in a transitional state. It had entered its scientific stage. The rigours and anomalies of the old law were stubbornly resisting the attempt made to simplify the Corpus Juris by harmonizing it into conformity with certain leading principles, and to pervade it with the milder tone, the cosmopolitan and levelling spirit, which these principles of the philosophical jurists brought from their origin in Stoicism. In the case of slavery the old system had at present a decided advantage over its assailants; since it had the double support of legal conservatism, and of the necessities, hereafter to be dwelt upon, of the existing social system. Thus when Christianity came in contact with the law the case stood thus, that slavery as an institution was intact, and so were many of its harsher incidents; but that a change had begun, and that certain small improvements had been achieved by the action of principles, which really demanded nothing less than abolition for their complete satisfaction, and were only kept at bay by the causes which made slavery a political necessity. Christianity took up the change and continued it, but she too failed to complete it; and when the Western Empire fell after a century and half of dominant Christianity, its slave laws bore at least as much trace of their original character, as of the modifications by which this has been softened. The most we can claim for Christianity is, that she pushed on the alterations with more vigour than had been the case before, and in ways which made them more effectual and beneficent.

We have therefore to see (α) what changes had already been achieved, (β) what Christianity added, (γ) what it left undone.

α. It is perhaps impossible, certainly difficult, to ascertain whether or in what degree the law felt Christian influences before the Emperors became Christian; for instance, in the great Antonine period. This difficulty will be avoided and the matter simplified here, if nothing is ascribed to Christianity, except those changes which were made after the period of Constantine.

The old theory which denied to the slave the simplest rights of a human being had been first invaded by Sulla, when he provided that the murder of a slave by a stranger should be considered as homicide, and not merely as an injury to the master's property; but the Lex Cornelia in no way affected the case in which the arbitrary power of his own master decreed the death of the slave. Against this, as against the same right which, we must admit, the father exercised over his own son, public feeling seems to have revolted from the earliest days of the Empire; but not till the time of Hadrian[e] and Antoninus[f] had the Emperors the

[e] Spart. Adr. 18.   [f] Quoted by Gaius, Dig. i. VI. 1.

humanity or courage to enact that a magistrate's sentence should be necessary, before a slave could be killed. The barbarous practice which cast aside the worn-out servant, as a broken or useless tool, was attacked by the two provisions of Claudius[g], which gave liberty to the sick slave whom his master had abandoned if he recovered, and punished the master as a homicide if he died. It was a step further when the Imperial legislation ventured to interfere with the ordinary relation of the slave and his master, and opened to hopeless misery a gate of relief. Antoninus[h] allowed that a slave who fled to the altar from his master's ill-treatment should not be restored, but be sold by the magistrate.

The rescript to Ælius Martianus, which contains this provision, deserves careful notice. It provides only for an extreme case; it takes care that the master shall be indemnified by the proceeds of the sale; but even then it seems hardly to dare allude to the slave, still less to appeal to considerations of humanity, in its anxiety to show that it is prompted only by regard for the master's interests. A sufficiently significant illustration of the condition of Roman opinion at the time, and of the powerlessness of nobler ideas to overcome a selfish and therefore cruel prejudice: yet incomplete, until it is added that the appointment by Nero, three-quarters of a century earlier, of an officer to watch over the treatment of slaves had not made such a remedy superfluous and impossible[i]. This is one of the cases not uncommon in the legislation upon this subject, in which the reiteration of a law shows its practical nullity and the resistance offered to it by public opinion, and so diminishes its historical importance.

Such another instance was the law of Hadrian[k], reenacted by Diocletian[l], which limited the application of torture to

---

g Cod. J. Lib. VII. v. sect. 3.   h Just. Inst. I. viii. 2.

i Senec. de Benef. III. 22.   Dig. I. xii. 1. sect. 1 & 5.

k Dig. XLVIII. xviii. 1 pr.   l Cod. Just. IX. xli. 8.

the slave. Simpler and easier methods of enfranchisement
exhibit the simplifying tendencies which inspired the philosophical jurists with an aversion of formalities. The Lex
Petronia[m], attributed diversely to Augustus and Nero, and
followed up by a law of[n] M. Aurelius, which forbade the
use of slaves for combats with the beasts, the prohibition
of Hadrian to employ them as gladiators, and the inference drawn by the jurisconsult from the rescript of
Antoninus above quoted, whereby they brought the case
of the application of a slave to labour for which he was
unfit, within the scope of the rescript, all helped the ameli-
oration of the slave's condition.

In a multitude of small questions which arose with regard
to status, the lawyers, in deference to their principle of
shewing "favour to liberty," gave a claim of freedom the
benefit of every doubt, and allowed to the "law of nature,"
in the decision of these narrower issues, the full play which
in the government of the whole question was denied to it.
The case where slaves, whom a will enfranchised, were
allowed to act as heirs, if no one else came forward to support the will, is one among many of the same sort. The
direct advantages thus gained were solid, though small; but
doubtless there was a greater indirect effect in the improvement of public opinion due to the habit of deferring to
liberal principles of the kind. The possibility that a slave
might in rare cases acquire not only liberty, but the position
of a freeborn man (*ingenuus*), shews what breaches these
principles had made in the old law. Such a slave was
restored to his natal condition. By this, said the lawyers,
is meant not the condition in which he was actually born,
viz. that of a slave; but the condition into which all men
are naturally born, viz. that of liberty[o]. The Roman
jurists had reached higher notions of humanity than the

[m] L. ii. §. 2. (Modest.) D. XLVIII. viii. Ad Leg. Cornel. de Sicariis.
[n] L. ii. §. 1. id. ib.   [o] Dig. XL. xi. 2.

moderns, who insist on natural differences of race. Certain
elementary family rights were obtained by the slave, as will
be mentioned in the next section: it was a great thing that
in legacies[p] and certain transactions, the wives and families
of the slaves are allowed to pass with them, and that, in
one case at least, from motives of humanity, the separation of families was recognized as a hardship and an
injustice[q].

Nevertheless, strange as it may seem, slavery was not
appreciably nearer its abolition. It would be wrong to
treat the modifications of detail above quoted as steps
towards the destruction of the institution, or as the con-
cessions by which an institution, consciously nearer its end,
compromises for its existence with public opinion.

β. Did Christianity achieve more complete success? The
answer will be disappointing. Christianity carried on the
changes, but she too left them incomplete, as a few instances will show.

The slave's condition is improving, he rises out of the
category of things, so soon as it is allowed that he can
engage in family relations. Constantine partly recognized
this when he forbade, in very distinct words, the separation
of families as a result of actions on partnership[r]; but the
same thing had been already done in what was probably a
more usual case, that of legacies. Also he allowed these
servile relationships to guide the succession in case the
persons related afterwards became free[s]; but before his time
they were so far recognized, as to be a bar to the intermarriage of persons so related. An equal penalty of death
for rape, whether committed upon a slave or free woman[t],
might seem to imply a high degree of respect for the rights

p Dig. XXXIII. vii. 12, 7.　　　q Dig. XXXII. 41. 2.
r Cod. Just. III. xxxviii. 11.
s Inst. III. vii. pr., " humanitate suggerente."
t Cod. J. IX. xiii. 1.

of our common human nature: the inference is checked
by the discovery that, spite of the protests of the Christians
and the declamations of Chrysostom, the adultery of a slave
woman was still no crime: as to them, says Constantine,
"vilitas vitæ dignas legum observatione non credidit[u]."
The restrictions on the use of torture begun in heathen
time were increased[x], but the practice was still employed.
The laws of Constantine[y], regulating the exercise of masters'
powers, shew clearly enough how futile past laws of the same
kind had been, and how little public opinion was even then
favourable to the cause of humanity. The edicts of the
Christian Emperor have little enough of the Christian spirit,
yet for centuries to come they remained the standing law
of the Christian Empire. The barbarity of the acts which
they proscribe is terrible; but perhaps the greatest barbarity
lies in the shortness of the catalogue. Take as proofs these
words, "si virgis aut loris servum dominus afflixerit........
nullum criminis metum mortuo servo sustineat."

In all these cases we see improvement, but no radical
change. Probably on the question of enfranchisement
Christianity won greatest successes: and enfranchisement
implied the permanence of the institution to which it introduced an exception. It could be performed in Churches:
the clergy could perform it anywhere[z]. By such enact-
ments Christianity secured the announcement in the most
formal possible way of the Christian character of these acts.
In the Lower Empire, if an inheritance reverted to the fire,
all the slaves comprised in it became free.

On specific points, such as the use of slaves for gladiatorial shows, for fights with beasts, for the vile purposes of
sensuality, for the degrading services of the theatre,
Christianity through the law strikes at abuses which she
hated with twofold hatred. The practices were abominable

[u] Cod. Th. IX. vii. 1.   [x] Cod. Theod. ix. 1. 14.
[y] Cod. Th. IX. xii. de Emend. Servorum.   [z] Cod. Th. IV. vii

to her, she declaimed against them, even when voluntarily
entered upon ; but they were doubly abominable when
maintained by compulsion. Yet in the gladiatorial shows
captives were employed to the last ; and Christian influence
only destroyed the shows through a deed of startling de-
votion—the gallant self-sacrifice of Telemachus in the fifth
century—leaving the fights with beasts to remain to the
end. Even in the extreme case of the "ludicra ministeria,"
Christianity was powerless to remove the stigma, which
degraded, both socially and morally, the wretched instruments of the public pleasures, or to abolish the displays
which needed instruments confessedly so vile. To these,
even hope was denied; they could not be enfranchised.
Christianity could not abolish the disability; she limited
her efforts, and, according to the general law, when con-
centrated they achieved more: for the female slave of the
theatre, (male gained no benefit from the law,) if converted
to Christianity, might be withdrawn from the stage[a]. By
rescuing Christians, the Church established her protest; and
the spirit of Christianity is naturally so liberal, that the
benefits conferred on her own members could hardly
become barriers of exclusion towards those without. So it
proved, for Leo[b] extended to all women, what his predecessor had granted to Christian women, that, without their
own consent, they could neither be put upon the stage nor
kept there. The objections to the stage were founded
mainly on grounds of morality. And the rescue of women
shows that the law had imbibed the spirit, and carried out
with some vigour the purposes, of Christianity. In the
same spirit is another law (one of 385 A.D.) forbidding
the training or sale of female slaves as musicians[c]. But
Christianity attempted further to secure the triumph which
it had won. In tracing the history of any progress, such,

[a] Cod. Theod. Lib. xv. VII. 4 and 8.   [b] Cod. J. Lib. i. IV. 14.
[c] Cod. Th. XV. vii. 10.

for instance, as that of constitutional freedom in England, the value of a concession, or a charter, is greatly enhanced by a guarantee for its observance. It was, therefore, a double victory for Christianity that the power of guaranteeing the laws relating to the slaves of the theatre was intrusted to her own officials. The extension of the laws was to be superintended by magistrates, " with the help and surveillance of the Bishop." This was not the only case to which such a guarantee was allowed. After the Empire became Christian, the confusion of spiritual and temporal functions soon began; and many duties were assigned by the Government to the Bishops, no doubt as being commonly the most trustworthy local officers. So in the case of the sale of slaves for prostitution, Constantine had already allowed ecclesiastics, or even prominent laymen, to rescue Christians at a fair price, when Theodosius and Valentinian, in 428, forbade any master so to use his power, under penalty of slavery in the mines; and provided, as a guarantee, that the slave so threatened might appeal to the Bishop[d]. Unfortunately, the inadequacy of the first law is proved by the passing of the second. Again, it was to the Bishop that Justin entrusted the power of freeing prisoners from those private prisons, destroyed[e] by his rescript, which were so connected with the horrors of slavery. Again, to the Bishop, Honorius[f] gave the right of guarding against a fraudulent abuse of the law, by which he allowed the finder of an exposed child to take him up and keep him as a slave. On this question of exposure Christianity was still awaiting its more signal triumph, when Justinian enacted that all children exposed, even though slave by birth, should be free[g]. Laws of tremendous

---

[d] Cod. Th. xv. 8. The words of this law show its source: " qui suis ancellis peccandi necessitatem inponunt." This is a Christian phrase.

[e] Cod. J. i. IV. 23. [f] Cod. Th. V. vii. 2.

[g] Cod. J. VIII. lii. 3.

severity against kidnappers showed the value which Christian and philosophical teaching had given to liberty, and by their side a harsh fugitive law seems the more odious.

This short view of the Christianized Imperial Law concerning slavery and some of its abuses, to which perhaps a desire not to seek lucidity by pressing the facts into an arrangement based on any preconceived theory, has given a somewhat desultory and unmethodical appearance, seems to confirm the view already taken. The Roman law, from its developed and elaborate character, detected and threw off with greater ease any foreign influence. It was, therefore, a hard battle which Christianity had to fight; and scarcely touching the main principles of the system, she was content with improvements of detail, themselves in part suggested or begun during the Pagan period.

γ. A recapitulation of the main features of the slave law of the Empire at the time of the barbarian invasion, will serve to prove this conclusion more irresistibly, and will conclude this part of the subject.

The slave, then, in the last days of the Imperial Jurisprudence had no rights of marriage: his 'contubernium' was still unrecognized by law; the slave woman could not commit adultery; the intermarriage of free and slave was still, in some cases at least, branded by stigma and penalty. The laws which checked the master's use of his authority over the slave left an arbitrary power of inflicting punishment so severe, that it was no surprise if the slave died from its effects. The courts of justice subjected him to torture in the trials to which he was summoned as a witness, while they denied to him, except in the single case of a claim to freedom, a plaintiff's rights to justice and protection. Male slaves might be forced to the still more debasing slavery of the public stage; and Honorius, in the last days of the

Roman Empire, seems to have repealed the edicts which saved women from the same doom.

Clearly, if we determine to rest the credit of Christianity or its effects upon the Roman Law, these last facts warn us that the claim must be moderate if it is to be successful[h].

Turning to the other aspect of the question in this earlier period, the difficulty of arriving at tangible results is greater. A statute book explains itself; even the amount of obedience which the laws receive may be fairly estimated from the frequency of their repetition. But a change in society, in manners, in morals, leaves behind no such definite records. Those who seek to trace it are perplexed by the various exaggerations of the zealous partizan who recounts the successes of his own party or his own generation; and of the querulous cynic who depreciates his contemporaries to justify either a general scepticism about human nature, or an invidious comparison with an ideal past. Yet such an enquiry is, for two reasons, most important. First, because laws are an imperfect index to the condition of society. A nation may be happy and free under laws the provisions of which seem harsh and unsatisfactory, while a system professedly liberal and fair may be so worked as to become, in fact, oppressive. Political and legal forms must be judged, not according to their letter, but in view of their actual working. Thus, e.g., harsh as the Pagan law of slavery was, we will undertake to say that by itself it would not reveal to any one the

[h] The laws of the Byzantine Empire, however, added some improvements; and these Laws are evidently Ecclesiastical in spirit. Basil and Alexius Comnenus sanctioned the marriage of slaves by the Christian rite. Leo allows them the free use of their peculium, and broke down some of the restrictions upon the intermarriage of slaves and free, turning such marriage into a source of freedom. The fisc under Basil and Constantine Porphyrogenitus refused to treat slaves as part of the profit which it derived from the death of intestate proprietors, and emancipated them. But still some points remained untouched: e.g. the incapacity of slaves as witnesses; and law seems to have been struggling with public opinion.

abomination of the slave system; and we suspect, on the other hand, that the legal improvements of the Christian period give a very inadequate idea of the improvement in the treatment of slaves, and in the state of public opinion with regard to them which Christianity produced in Christianized Rome. Secondly, this is the sphere in which Christianity is most at home. Her genuine office, her natural place is that of the still small voice which pleads from within with the hearts of men; or, if she appears in public, it is as the preacher who arraigns men at no tribunal but that of God and of their own conscience, and speaks with no authority but that of Religion and Truth.

It must be remarked in a prefatory way, that, in the period at present under consideration, Christianity passed through changes, both of fortune and of character, perhaps more rapid than those which at any other time she has undergone. At first the Church contained a small body, outcasts from society for the sake of religion, whose sincerity was put to constant proof by the test of persecution. But after a time persecution ceased; the Emperors became Christian; the hitherto hostile influences of fashion and high example were now ranged on the side of Christianity. From henceforth the action of the Church, which had been that of a single-hearted body full of almost inspired earnestness, took a new character. The voice of sincere believers was partly drowned, and their action impeded, by the crowd of half-hearted and worldly converts. These professed members, while they cared little for the principles and doctrines of Christianity, cared much for the system to which they owed wealth, luxury, and power. Recruited from such materials, the Church's action became less steady, her protests less indignant and energetic, the inclination to compromise with prevailing tastes or institutions grew stronger, political prudence cooled the glow of missionary zeal; and, if her dominant position gave her surveillance, moral and religious, over society at large, yet in its diffusion her influence became less impetuous and effective. These reflections throw light on what has gone before, and we are reminded that the Christianity which casts its influence upon the law was the Christianity of the fourth, and not of the first, century,—Imperial, rather than Apostolic, in its temper. In regard to what follows, they indicate that statements with regard to the influence of Christianity upon society within the Empire must be qualified according as they are applied to the earlier or later parts of the Imperial period: the guiding rule being this, that in the early period its influence is more un-adulterated; in the latter, more extensive in its scope.

In the primitive days, evidence need hardly be sought. If a common worship has been deemed likely to remind the Christian master of his brotherly relation to his slave, how much more would it be so when that worship implied a risk of martyrdom, performed secretly in the catacomb or cave in order to avoid the persecutor's notice! The de-pendence on a common Father's love and care could not then be forgotten. With death constantly before their eyes, suffering together for the same Lord, the distinction of earthly ranks must have sunk into utter insignificance. The ideal picture which imagination would thus draw is realized in the facts as they are preserved to us. It is surpassed in the sublimely loving and tender pleading of the Epistle to Philemon. In that Epistle, the first docu-ment of Ecclesiastical History on this subject, St. Paul does not forget to refer to his own imprisonment, and to the affectionate relations into which it had brought him with the slave Onesimus, as a ground on which to base his plea that Onesimus may be treated with the love and con-sideration due to a brother in Christ. Or passing to uninspired Christians, what can realize more vividly the way in which Christianity dissolved all the evil and misery

of slavery, than the touching story of Perpetua and Feli-
citas, the noble matron and the poor ancilla sharing
together the troubles and joy of martyrdom, sustained by
one another's love; or that of Blandina, the slave of Vienne,
whose voice, in the midst of her agonies, animated the
courage of her highborn fellow-sufferers, with whom she
had been associated by the persecutors for the increase of
their ignominy. Nor were these cases exceptional: Christianity in its despised beginnings was no luxury, like Stoicism, of the higher classes, or of those few among the slaves
who, being possessed of some education, were employed for
higher purposes, and least needed defence and consolation.
The case was rather the other way. It was the hackneyed
reproach of the Church, made, for instance, by Celsus[i], that
its members were of the viler sort: translated, as Origen
replies[k], that reproach means that the privileges and consolations of Christianity were brought home to the most
miserable and the most hopeless. In the same spirit, and
for the same reason, Origen defends Christianity against the
taunt levelled by the cultivated heathen, at the absence of
taste, the rudeness and simplicity which characterized its
manner of teaching. By that simplicity, he answers, it
has done what philosophers never did: they taught truth
to the few, Christianity has made it the property of mankind. Its doctrine exercises the faculties of the highest
intellect: it is intelligible to the meanest slave. It was this
universal character which Gnostic and Manichæan exclusiveness would have destroyed.

These passages from early Church History suggest one
aspect of the present question common to all periods, on
which it may be well to say a word once for all. In treat-
ing of slavery men are apt to dwell too exclusively upon
the conduct of masters, and to scrutinize only the treatment
to which by law or custom they subject the slave. The

---

i Orig. cont. Cels. III. 50.   k Orig. cont. Cels. III. 54.

condition of the slave himself is often neglected : and the
reason being that it is harder to obtain statistics or information. So in action, when benevolence takes up the
slave's cause, more stress is laid upon the attempt to control
and mitigate the master's despotism, than upon schemes for
elevating the condition moral and spiritual of the slave himself. Yet this is surely the higher object : the end for the
sake of which other changes are valuable as means. If it is
harder to trace, this is not because the effects are less real ;
but because they operate in the nobler, that is, the invisible,
parts of man, his mind and spirit. It is a great thing to
alleviate misery, and to raise the degraded : but it is far
greater to infuse into the human soul that which makes it
triumph over misery, and turn its degradation by spiritual
victory into its discipline and its boast. The influence of
Christianity has been, and in this Essay no attempt is made
to disguise the fact, sometimes and in some respects over-
rated : but it is no exaggeration to say that the triumph
over slavery in the heart of the slave is a victory which she
alone has either won, or attempted to win. By the magic
of her influence she has transmuted that which was a badge
of vileness, and a sign of exclusion from every high and
animating hope, into a discipline in which the soul of the
faithful slave finds wherewithal to fit itself for immortal
destinies of glory. That which was once a vista of vacant
and painful drudgery, closed only by a death of extinction,
is now but one form of the thankful service which His
intelligent creatures pay to God, until He transfers them
to a higher service in the courts of Heaven. As we analyse
fully alterations in the law the improvements effected by
Christianity may seem to elude our grasp : with the declamations of the later fathers before us we may begin to
grow sceptical about the positive influence which it exercised
upon the morality and humanity of the slave-holding classes :
but the change which carried human souls across the gulf

which divides the ignominious and despised condition of the
Roman slave from the inward exaltation of Onesimus or
Blandina remains unimpeachable in evidence and historically
unique, the greatest moral miracle ever worked by purely
spiritual forces, unassisted by any change in circumstance
or external condition.

The Christianity of the Empire owed this success to the
imitation of her Master's example. She began as He had
begun, from the poor. They were established in the full
privileges of membership before the Churches included many
of the richer converts, who brought in with them some of
their exclusive prejudices. But as this was the greatest
triumph of Christianity, and implied the greatest exertion
of spiritual energy to overcome the influence of all other
forces, social and external, it was natural that it should be
soonest tarnished, and that the decrease of life within the
Church should show itself early in the failure fully to maintain before high and low the standard of spiritual equality.
Hence in the Empire the respect of persons, of which even
an Apostle has to complain, must have increased in the
Church: much more was it so in the Middle Ages. For,
in the second period of conversion, the old rule was inverted
and conversion began from the top. The vassals followed
the king into the font, and were in turn imitated by their
own followers. Thus the Church wore an aristocratic character, and the conversion of the peasantry, among whom
heathen customs long lingered, was a very different thing
from the admission of the Roman slaves into the close
brotherhood of the Primitive Church. Yet in a degree
Christianity still did its holy work among those whom man
despised; and among the lost pages of ecclesiastical history
there are many which would contain the unobtrusive and
unrecorded labours of the parish priests, themselves esteemed
little higher than their flocks, to make the precepts and
consolations of Christianity realities to the poor.

Will it be said, that, judged by its modern history, Christianity is powerless to raise the condition of those whom other influences degrade and depress; that it becomes to them little more than a form of hysterical excitement? It might be replied, that the circumstances were particularly unfavourable, since the negro race was one which demanded the highest missionary skill and energy, while the Church of the seventeenth and eighteenth centuries was specially destitute of such qualities: or, that the charge is not entirely true, witness such attempts as those of the Quakers in Barbados in the seventeenth century, under whose Christian influence sober and civilized congregations were rapidly formed. But the simplest answer is, that Christianity was not a free agent: it was often banished by the planters, as in the case of these Quakers, whose benevolent schemes were abruptly terminated, and they themselves forbidden the island: or, if admitted, it was fettered by their control. A slave-holding class is quick to see a revolutionary tendency in anything which raises the slaves in character and self-respect; and the planters, who forbade instruction in reading, suspected danger from the spiritual equality which Christianity taught. Nor were they far wrong: for such was the slavery which they maintained, that if Christianity had been allowed to awaken in the slaves the least sense of the rights and dignity of man, the least spark of the indignation which kindles at their violation, Christianity herself could hardly have preached resignation and submission with success. With the planters, therefore, or at worst with the "respectable" religion of the planter class, and not with Christianity, lies the responsibility of the negro's continued degradation. The separate worship of free and slaves, the official attendance of a single white as an overseer at the worship offered to a God with whom is no distinction of bond or free, the signal for prayers given by the whip, the slave-auction following by public announcement " at the

end of Mass," these indicate the causes which have made
Christianity fail to raise the slave in his own eyes and in the
respect of others. This is the dark side of the picture, and
the dark side almost covers the canvass; but there is room
for hope, that in spite of every obstacle the irresistible influence of Gospel Truth here and there filtered through,
and where the Bible was allowed, and instruction in reading
not prohibited, reached the hearts of some   ·

> " Who touched God's right hand in the darkness,
> And were lifted up and strengthened."

But to return. The Primitive Church had thus raised
the spiritual dignity of the slave as a member of Christ's
body, in his own, and in others' eyes. Time passed on, and
the Church entered on its more worldly period: yet the
Fathers hardly allowed the Apostolic teaching to degenerate
in their hands. Perhaps they are sometimes more anxious
than the New Testament writers to justify the existence of
slavery. Basil[1], for instance, seems almost to borrow *totidem
verbis* Aristotle's argument, which treats slavery as a benefit
to the slave. But this anxiety was itself a proof of their
increasing consciousness that the system was inconsistent
with Christianity. And nothing can be more lofty than
the view which they conceive of the behaviour and of
the relations of masters and slaves one toward another.
Addressing a public opinion professedly Christian, they
wrought out with wonderful fulness and breadth the bearing
of Christian doctrine upon the position of the slave. Ambrose[m] and Augustine[n] appealed to the old name of pater-
familias, Chrysostom[o] reminded the mistress that her slave
is also her sister: if slavery is to exist among Christians, at
least, they all agree, it must involve no forgetfulness of those
other and higher ties, not of property or service, but of

[1] De Spiritu Sancto, xx.   [m] Ep. I. ii. 31. (ed. Migne.)
[n] De Civ. Dei, xix. 16. (ed. Migne.)
[o] ἀδελφὴ σού γέγονεν εἰ ᾖ πιστή. ad Eph. IV. Homil. xv.

brotherhood and love, of common service and common son-
ship, which unite the master and the slave, and be disfigured
by no conduct incompatible with such relationship [p]. Like
the Apostles too, they give these precepts their twofold
application. They enjoin tenderness and care on the
masters; but they also exhort the slaves to be active for
conscience sake in the freewill service which is really
freedom.

There was in all this a double novelty. First, the teaching itself was superior, by all the interval which separates
Stoicism from Christianity, to anything which had gone
before; its principles more deep and exhaustive, its exhortations more definite and moving. But a greater novelty,
if possible, was the machinery which gave the teaching
vogue and influence. It was possible to speak publicly
to large mixed congregations, and it was possible to speak
with the authority of doctrines to which all were bound
by their profession to shew respect. The manners and
opinions of the day were tried by an acknowledged standard,
and the preacher might rouse the conscientious and shame
the indifferent by denunciation of the abuses which belied
the common Christianity. The pulpit was a new power;
and it is interesting to observe that much of the teaching
of the Fathers is contained in their homilies and sermons.
It would be a paradox to maintain that a public opinion
so challenged was not in some degree elevated by the pro-
cess. The declamations of Chrysostom against the abuses
of Byzantine society may cost him his see, but the hatred
of the people shewed that he had reached their consciences;
and while the many expelled the preacher, some few would
profit by his lessons.

It is necessary to lay some stress on the fact that this
must have been so, because when the question arises in
what degree did an improvement actually shew itself; how

[p] Ambr. ut sup.; he adds, "quasi animæ consortes." cf. Apost. Const. iv. 12

far did practice at all correspond to the lofty ideal which the Church proclaimed, the positive evidence seems to be weak. In all such matters the negative cases are always the easiest to find : lives of quiet obedience to duty pass unnoticed and unrecorded, while the memory of the bad is preserved in the denunciations which they elicit. But we have certain recorded instances in the works of Jerome, whose correspondence was the fruit of an intercourse with a very large part of the Christian society of his time, of mistresses who treated their slave-women in a Christian spirit, joining in their occupations; so that, according to his strong expression in one case[q], the mistress could hardly be singled out from among the slaves about her. Chrysostom[r] "knew" himself "many houses which had gained much from the virtue of their slaves." Manumission, and that of large numbers at a time, became a popular act of piety ; it was made the subject of a special exemption in the laws which forbade legal transactions upon Sunday[s]. Masters were to see that their slaves had been baptized[t]; and the Church declined, with magnanimous confidence in the master's uprightness, to baptize any one without his consent, assuming that this would not be withheld except for reasons which also disqualified for the rite[u]. They were responsible for the religious instruction of their slaves, and their attendance on divine worship. Chrysostom, in one of his sermons, bade the members of his congregation adopt the practice of reading to their households from some sacred book, and allow the slaves to listen. "Make a church of your house," he cried[x]; and the acclamations

q Hieron. Ep. xxiii. ed. Migne.

r In 2 Ep. ad Thess. Homil. v. 3. ed Migne.

s Cod. Theod. II. viii. de Feriis. i. As other business on Sundays is 'indignissumum : ita gratum et jucundum est codie quæ maxime sint votiva compleri: atque ideo emancipandi, &c.'

t Cod. Justin.　　　　　u Const. Apost. viii. 32. (Labbe i. 495 D.)

x 'Εκκλησίαν ποίησον σοῦ τὴν οἰκίαν, in Genes. Serm. vi. 2.

with which his hearers greeted[y] his epigrammatic phrase
shewed that at least in their better moments their hearts
responded to the call. It was perhaps in part for the same
reason that the Apostolical Constitution secured rest for
the slave on Saturdays, Sundays, and the great days and
seasons of the Church[z]. The Church might hope by throw-
ing these duties on the masters to make them realize more
vividly their Christian responsibilities[a]. The authority of
the Bishops, who were now both by law and custom the
recognized defenders of all helpless and oppressed classes,
often interposed for the protection of the slave. In the
73rd and 74th letters of S. Basil[b] a case of this kind occurs.
S. Basil pleads with admirable tact and courtesy (he must
have studied the Epistle to Philemon to good effect) for
certain slaves who had committed an offence and then
sought his protection. He asks that they may be spared
and left to him for moderate chastisement.

The slave might avail himself of the privileges of sanctuary to defend himself from injury: and though law, secular
and ecclesiastical, required the consent of the master before
a slave could enter a monastery or take Orders, yet three
years in one case and one in the other was sufficient to
establish a prescription in favour of liberty[e], and we may
reflect without much compunction that the Church was
probably not too careful in observing the restriction which
guarded the master's rights. If consent had been given
he became free at once: the holy place raised its silent
protest against the system.

Again, the care of the early Church for the poor and
distressed must have included the slaves[d], since they con-

---

[y] v. the Sermon of the next day, in Genes. Serm. vii. 1.
[z] Const. Apost. viii. 33.
[a] v. the whole tone of the passage in the Civ. Dei, xix. 15, 16.
[b] Migne Patrol. vol. xxxii. 439—443.
[c] Just. Nov. v. 2. 1, and cxxiii. 17.   [d] cf. C. Just. VII. vi. 3.

stituted so large a portion of the lower orders. This took
its first form in the community of goods providing a
common treasury, whence the deacons distributed daily
ministrations to the widows. It reappears in the collec-
tions for the poor saints, about which St. Paul, in the
midst of his spiritual duties, is so much occupied : it suggested a subject for Lucian's cynicism, in the retinue of
widows and orphans who wait upon their Christian bene-
factor [e]: Julian recognized it by his imitation in the pagan
revival ; it embraced in a degree those outside the Christian
pale ; it founded in the more settled days of the Church a
whole range of institutions for the relief of the distressed ;
and it acquires and retains throughout Mediæval History a
formal and legal shape in that third part of the tithes and
other customary offerings which the Bishop was bound to
administer to the poor. It is useless, where space is short,
to accumulate the proofs of this charitable action of Christianity. It is only needful to remark that the slaves must
have received benefit from it, and that others were saved
by it from slavery.

One form of charity peculiarly connected with slavery—
the redemption of captives, the slaves who felt slavery
most—will be mentioned again, in connection with the time
at which it becomes most important, and is alluded to here
only in order to refer to a single conspicuous instance of it
belonging to the present period, in which Cyprian [f] writing
in behalf of some African captives makes appeal in a very
remarkable manner to the great presiding doctrines of Christianity, whose application to slavery was partly shewn in the
earlier part of this Essay.

The denunciations of the Fathers against the games, the
theatre, the practice of exposing infants, were all so many
attacks upon sources or aggravations of slavery.

[e] Lucian Peregrinus, cap. xii. Pressensé H. des 3 Prém. Siécles 2 série
ii. 99.   [f] Ep. lx.

But, in point of fact, draw out as we may the beneficial influences of Christianity, they can hardly be comprehended without fully realizing the condition of Roman society. No description of that society can be given here : suffice it to indicate, that among its prominent characteristics were the two which are at all times the most fruitful parents of cruelty—sensuality and panic; and that it owed both to slavery. It was sensual, because the person of slaves was at the mercy of their masters, and because they ministered to the most extravagant and sensualizing luxury. It was panic-stricken, because they were numerous and disaffected, gathered from all countries, and bound to the governing classes by no ties of sympathy or interest[g]. Men said that if a peculiar dress had been allowed to disclose to the slaves their own numbers, the revelation would have imperilled the State[h]. This ever-present alarm was invoked to justify, and can alone now explain, the vote by which the most august assembly of Rome, turning a deaf ear to the pleas of "sex, age, and undoubted innocence," sacrificed, by a judicial murder, 400 slaves of a master whom one of the number had assassinated. Without that explanation, a modern reader would draw even exaggerated inferences from cruelty so detestable, not confined to a single instance or due to special reasons, but repeated as a common practice, sanctioned and regulated, as extant[i] documents prove, by the authority of the laws. But explanation does not affect the inferences which the practice suggests as to the condition of the society in which it is found. Our conception of it will be more complete when we remember that the cruelty, which fear prompted and sensuality fostered, was whetted and brutalized by the bloody scenes of the arena,

[g] Postquam nationes in familiis habemus, quibus diversi ritus externa sacra aut nulla sunt, colluviem istam nonnisi metu coërcueris. Tac. Ann. xiv. 44.

[h] Senec. de Clem. I. 24.

[i] v. S. C. Silanianum and Paul's comment S. III. v. 6.

and in a sceptical and materialistic age was unchecked by any sanctions of a settled religion or a settled morality.

A glance at this horrible picture seems to supply two hints for a right judgment upon this part of the question. First, it confirms the belief already expressed, that Christianity cannot but have worked much improvement. It was impossible for men to flatter themselves that all was well with society; every zealous Christian must have been fired by such a state of things to attempt some reform; and such efforts cannot have been wholly vain. But, secondly, it explains the existence of the darker side of the picture, which has still to be drawn. For, speaking generally, under the Christianized Empire the whole of the society just described entered the Church. What material for Christianity to mould! A society in the last stage of corruption, and whose corruption seemed to flow, as an inevitable consequence, from its political and economical condition! Tacitus had said of it, in hackneyed words, that it could neither bear its evils nor their remedies; and its history to the end justified his prophecy. How certain that the Christian standard must infinitely degenerate! — that the ministers of Christianity would struggle vainly against the overwhelming flood of evil: that an ideal of conduct, which implied the highest triumph of grace and Christian forbearance in both master and slave, should be hopelessly neglected; and that, spite of a few faithful souls whose now-forgotten lives preserved the traditions of the Primitive Church, the general conduct should compel us to the verdict that Christianity failed to regenerate the slavery of the Roman Empire.

Here, alas! there is no difficulty in obtaining the evidence. The real difficulty is, to distinguish the Christian society from its Pagan predecessor. We have to remind ourselves that the good has often left no record, and that Christianity probably had more influence in the households,

which contained a few slaves for necessary service, than in
the palaces of the great. In these, everything seems un-
changed: the Christian master still rules his hosts of slaves
for every conceivable purpose of service, luxury, or display;
(could he be to them what S. Paul wished Philemon to be
to Onesimus?) the taste for eunuchs witnesses to a degraded
morality, the fantastic curiosity which paid high prices for
dwarfs and monsters to hearts hardened by luxury and
sensuality. S. Chrysostom confirms these inferences by
his direct testimony. He declaims against the numbers of
slaves: he thunders against their treatment. Take a single
one of his Sermons[k]. He speaks of the cruelty of women
towards their female slaves. They accost them with every
term of obscenity and reproach; they expose them naked
to be flogged by their husbands; they uncover their heads,
and drag them by their hair; and for all this they dare to
set up pleas of defence. The allusion to the cries which
attract the passers by in the street below, seems to set this
before us as a sketch from the every day life of the capital.
We must hope that the blush which covered the faces of his
hearers[l], if in many it was the sign of a guilty conscience,
yet showed that there were some who listened with shame
and indignation to the description of conduct so atrocious.
A word from Jerome suffices to show the state of morality
which slavery still produced. The female slave was too low
for virtue, "passim per ancillulas libido permittitur[m]."

Or turn to the slaves themselves. The Fathers confess
that they are guilty of every vice and every crime: pro-
fligate, thieving, treacherous, brutish. Only they asked[n],
and history repeats the question, how could they be otherwise? How could they learn the duties and temper of

[k] ad Eph. iv. Hom. XV.
[l] τί ἠρυθριάσατε πᾶσαι; ad Eph. iv. Hom. XV.
[m] Hieron. Ep. LXXVII. 3. ed Migne.
[n] Cf. Chrys. in Ep. ad Eph. v. Hom. XX.

Christian slaves, when their masters had so entirely forgotten the corresponding obligations; when cruelty and
contempt destroyed their self-respect, and neglect deprived
them of access to Christianity[o]? As it was, even the Fathers
could not help countenancing the use of the rod and
scourge[p]. A Christian system of slavery would have
bound the slaves in close allegiance to their masters, and,
through them, to the State; but when Alaric approached
Rome the slaves deserted to him by thousands.

The sight of this condition of society suggests the
question, why there had been so little change, and why the
latent tendencies of Christianity towards abolition had borne
no fruit.

The first cause was fear. The authority of masters was,
in fact, the police which kept in order a large, fierce, and
disaffected population. As in the Slave States of America,
the citizens were few among many, and were united by no
ties to their subjects. Christianity had offered to furnish a
bond of union and sympathy; but the offer had been rejected, and it was only too true, that if the strong hand of
power had relaxed its grasp, there were no other restraints
to which it was safe to trust.

The second was the depreciation of free labour. This
was partly due to the opportunities for money-making opened
by commerce, foreign service, and provincial appointments;
partly to the ancient contempt for handicraft, which, in
consequence of these openings, all the citizens could afford
to share; partly to the drain of men for military purposes:
it was completed by the cheapness of slave labour, which
the increasing dearth of free men willing to work made it
necessary to employ, and of which incessant war and conquest insured an economical supply. When labour had

---

[o] Chrys. ad Eph. VI, Hom. xxii.

[p] Ῥάβδῳ καὶ πληγαῖς σωφρόνισον. Chrys. ad Eph. IV. Homil. xv. Seu
verbo seu verbere. Aug. de Civ. Dei, xix. 16.

thus been consigned to slaves, the old contempt for it increased; and so it came about that no one would work who was not obliged, and that slavery was a necessary institution. The character of the freed-men of the Empire was not likely to encourage emancipationist schemes. All this applies most truly to domestic slavery; for, during the times of the Empire, a gradual change in economical conditions was raising the agricultural slave-gangs to the rank which is just above that of the slave, namely, the colonate. But this was not the result of Christianity; and some of the characteristics of slavery, to which Christianity was most opposed, attached to the colonus.

The third reason was the influence of traditional ideas. Slavery always had existed. As has been seen, the Roman lawyers said that it was sanctioned by the *jus gentium;* in other words, it was one of the customs common to all nations. To the Romans it had been handed down with the institutions which, for want of something better, they almost literally worshipped; and no doubt, to a Roman, slavery seemed as natural and necessary as the relation of master and servant, employer and employed, seems now. In the ancient case, as in the modern, a few speculators might question this. Chrysostom, to pursue the parallel, might hint at an ideal society, founded on a communistic interchange of services[q], as now men talk of a social state, based on cooperation; but then, as now, the ordinary run of men had no doubts about the necessity and permanence of the existing state of things.

For these reasons, among others, Christianity did not achieve a result which it never set itself directly to attempt, and which, if it had been achieved, would have been the effect of the slow operation of its doctrines and their consequences in the minds of men, viz. the abolition of slavery; and the general proposition, which was assumed at the

q ad Eph. Hom. xix. 141.

outset, seems to be verified in the case of Rome, viz. that Christianity affects slavery by mitigating its rigours; and not, unless other influences concur, by abolishing the institution.

In the earlier part of this Essay, two propositions have been advanced. First, that Christianity does not, unless under exceptional circumstances, abolish slavery, but only mitigates it. Secondly, that this mitigation is effected more by the complete triumph of Christian principles in a limited number of cases, than by their diffusive influence over society at large.

The first of these is verified by the history of Roman society; and the second derives special support from a history in which striking examples of self-denial and love stand out to rebuke, by striking contrast, the general selfishness and cruelty of society.

(ii) It is necessary to apply the same generalizations more briefly to the test of Mediæval History. For continuity's sake, the order of this part of the subject shall be altered, and the question which was asked last in the case of Roman slavery shall be put first here. What were the causes which maintained slavery, and prevented Christianity from abolishing it until they had themselves ceased to act?

In point of fact this question is part of the larger one, which seeks the explanation of the many relations of dependence and inferiority which are covered by the word feudalism. If one might venture to describe briefly a feudalized society, it would be in some such way as this: that it was the product of a period in which there was no balance of forces. It is to an equipoise that order and freedom are commonly due; if one force becomes overpowerly predominant, the men who can wield it are sure to become oppressors: and this, true at all times, is true especially of such a period as that of which

we speak, when violence was universal and unchecked by
the traditions of an established society. For self-defence
against violence, each man needed the command of some
force, and there was but one kind available, which was
monopolized by the few. Ordinarily wealth, intellectual
ability, spiritual power, represent each of them a social
force; and the force of numbers is generally lodged with
those who are destitute of the other kinds. But intellect
was not a force, for, at a time when there were no learned
professions, and when want of communications and igno-
rance prevented the existence of a public opinion on which
intellect might build its power, wealth could not supply
force to a great middle class of merchants or traders, for
insecurity made commerce and industry as yet impossible.
Spiritual powers did indeed assure authority and influence
to those who possessed them : but their voice was often un-
heard amid the stormy violence and the uncontrolled ferocity
of semibarbaric times. The total failure of such insurrec-
tions of the villeins as that which occurred in Normandy in
about 1000 A.D., shews that, in a time of proof armour,
the mass of the people drew as little strength for the phy-
sical superiority of numbers, as they did from the yet
unknown of doctrines of the rights of labour. No, there
was but one kind of force in society : the small number of
men who found themselves in possession of a stone castle,
a landed estate, and a band of dependents whom the land
would feed, had society at their mercy. The poorer men of
their own rank became their vassals, and were treated with
some consideration due to the fact that they constituted the
sinews of the lord's power : the first beginnings of a mer-
chant class submitted to be plundered by one lord that he
might protect them against the rest. Even the Church
(though in her case there is another side to the picture)
had in great measure to bow before the dominant class :

her great corporations, the cathedrals or the monasteries, admitted under the soft names of 'Advocacy' or protection, the interference and rapacity of the Seigneur: her individual clergy, ordained from the lowest classes, find their place as mass-chaplains, despised and without authority, among the retainers at the lower end of the baronial hall[r].

Is there here no explanation of mediæval serfdom? What was the fate of the poor man when even classes above him in the social scale were dependent on the nobility? He had less force than they; he must sink into a subjection still more complete. He became the serf whose labour, property, and person were placed at the arbitrary disposal of the lord. Thus mediæval serfdom was so necessary a consequence of the principle, so to call it, on which society was built, it was so intimately connected and matched so nicely with the other institutions of the period, that neither Christianity nor any other power could abolish it. The system was built by the selfishness, avarice, and violence of the barbarian conquerors and the aristocracies which they founded; and these are faults so universal among mankind that Christianity, though she may battle with them, can never overcome them in society at large. When once built, the system was too coherent and too strong to be assailed.

Christianity then did not abolish serfdom in the early middle ages. The above description was vague as to date. It was intended to delineate features which were more or less characteristic of all the European nations from the sixth to the twelfth centuries. To dispose of this part of the subject, nothing remains but to deal with the suggestion that Christianity did abolish serfdom, because in the interval between the thirteenth and the fifteenth or sixteenth centuries serfdom disappeared. It might well be answered, that this implies one of two assumptions equally paradoxical,—

[r] Agobard of Lyons De Privilegio et Jure Sacerdotii, c. 11. Ducange vi. 224.

either that the Christianity of the Avignonese Papacy acquired suddenly in the fourteenth century the power to
do what that of Gregory I. and the German Missionaries in
the sixth and seventh had failed to accomplish; or, that
Christianity laboured for seven or eight centuries at a pro-
gressive reformation, of which for three quarters of that
time there is not a tittle of historical evidence. But in fact
the idea is chimerical, since serfdom declined with the causes
which gave it birth.

Those causes have been assigned above; and if it has
been truly alleged that serfdom resulted from the monopoly
of force by a single class, then it would disappear in proportion as counteracting forces gathered strength, and the
helpless parts of society acquired the means of self-assertion
and self-defence. Now the history of Mediæval Europe,
from a period such as that of the Crusades, displays a
development of this kind, the rise of new political and
social forces, and the consequent redistribution of the power
once engrossed by the nobility alone. Every one knows
the causes of this change. From the time of the first
Crusade inter-communication becomes more frequent, commerce rises, the towns obtain privileges, wars are waged on
a larger scale by more extensive combinations. Learning
becomes a power, and the man of ability or education, whatever his birth, finds his sphere, either in the chair of a
University crowded by students of all countries, or as a
lawyer, the counsellor and supporter of the king. Abelard
and Gratian are contemporaries. The change was universal;
in a thousand ways it affected the lower classes: four may
be selected. First, the middle classes acquired power through
money, they broke down exclusive privileges, and to some
extent they secured an equal law, the benefits of which were
not unfelt by the peasantry. Secondly, the rule which
established that serfs residing a year and a day in a town
became free, made the rise of the cities a great boon to the

serfs; the lords felt that they must be careful in their treatment of those whom despair might drive to seek even a perilous means of escape. Thirdly, it is plain that as the noble proprietors were called upon to make increasing efforts to maintain their position, they were led to tend more carefully all the sources of their power. True, this very cause would have made them averse to emancipation, which was equivalent to the surrender of so much property. But then serfdom did not come to an end by way of emancipation. The history of copyhold tenures shows that it faded away gradually and imperceptibly, the whole class slowly rising in privilege and consideration, and coming to possess as right what had been granted to them as favours. And the anxiety of the lords to propitiate and attach them must have been fruitful of these boons. Lastly, with the change in the methods of warfare, the lower classes acquired a fighting value*: their importance was increased, and their spirit raised. Witness the intimate relation between the French wars and the insurrection of Wat the Tyler.

On the whole there is no case in history in which it is more certain that a great change has been the outcome not of any single cause or agency, but of the general movement and progress of society.

Christianity then upon this reasoning was not able in the mediæval any more than in the ancient times to " affect slavery" by abolishing it. As in the earlier case, its influence was mainly displayed in its power to modify and mitigate the harsher features of the institution which it was compelled to tolerate.

(1) In the crisis of transition from ancient to modern history, the sudden and piteous vicissitudes of fortune which accompany conquest stimulated into fuller activity a form of charity which Christianity had never neglected, and for which, during the centuries immediately preceding, border

* On the connection of fighting power and political influence, v. Ar. Pol.

raids and partial incursions of the barbarian tribes had provided an ample sphere[t]. This was the redemption of captives, a virtue never more necessary than at a time when
those who had been brought up in wealth and comfort were
liable to be suddenly overwhelmed by the miseries of captivity, and one with which the biographers of the sixth
century saints specially delight to adorn their heroes.
" Gratias agamus," says S. Germanus, " divinæ clementiæ
nam unde fiat redemptio appropinquavit." " How often,"
says the biographer of S. Eligius, " would he become a debtor
himself, that he might rescue those who were in debt[u]!" For
this purpose no sacrifice was too costly. Ambrose had
deprecated the blame which his enemies had thrown upon
his pious sacrilege to the sacred vessels, when he needed
their price to pay for redemption : the redemption of captives,
he had said, will be the ornament of the mysteries[x]. So in
the same spirit the Council of Rheims, held in 625[y], made
one exception to its injunction to preserve the sacred vessels.
" Nisi evenent," it says, " ardua necessitus pro redemptione
captivorum." It is wrong, says another authority, to allow
" anything, *even, in a great strait, the preservation of sacred
property*," to interfere with the constant exercise of this
duty. There were instances of a yet higher sacrifice, when
a man sold himself for another's redemption. The Council
of Orleans in 511[z], and after three centuries the Council of
Aachen in 816[a], mention this as one of the objects of the
possession of property by the Church. As has been said,
Christianity has in every age repeated this charitable practice. For completeness' sake it may be well to quote here,
from different periods, the story of Otto, the apostle of
Pomerança in the twelfth century, who redeemed captives

[t] Ozanam. Civ. du 5me. Siècle, ii. 41. Eng. Trans.
[u] Scr. Gall. III. 381, 385, 552.
[x] De Off. Ministr. ii. 28, 138. ed. Migne.
[y] Harduin. iii. 574 A. Can. XXII.   [z] Harduin. ii. 1009. Can. V.
[a] Harduin. iv. 1132 A. Can. 116.

E

as one way of exhibiting his Christianity to the heathen [b],—the practice connected with the Crusades of redeeming Christians from the Mussulman ; the redemption of Indian serfs by Las Casas; and of the slavegangs of South Africa in our own day by Mackenzie.

(2) But, to return, in spite of what individuals might do to soften the shock, to rescue some whom in the anarchy of society nothing but the placid spirit of Christian charity would have saved, the change was nevertheless accomplished, and new societies were formed, in which the arrogance of class was increased by the antipathy of race and the insolence of conquerors. Any one who would appreciate the plan of the battle which in these societies the Church had to fight afresh on behalf of the slaves, must have the character of the times vividly before him. The governing classes were barbarians, among whose force was almost the only power, and spiritual influences took the form of superstitious terrors acting violently but fitfully. They were Christians, but Christianity had not yet softened their characters, or moulded their ideas : their minds were not yet open to its pure principles, its genuine spiritual influence. Nor would they have accorded deference to a clergy which, destitute of the external symbols and instruments of power, should have claimed reverence in virtue of the spiritual powers and truths which it possessed and represented. The Church accommodated itself to the contingency : it put on the armour of the times, and it coped with this wild aristocracy of chiefs by transforming its own great officers into the character of secular lords. They acquired lands and retinue ; they became a powerful political order; and by their judicious use of this political force, so no doubt the best of them hoped, as well as by the skilful employment of the superstitious terrors which awed even the irreligious, they intended to advance the interests of true Christianity.

[b] Neander, vii. 16 and 24. Eng. Trans.

The result in some degree corresponded to the expectation. But the Church, when it adopted a secular position, was invaded by a secular spirit: and while she acquired new powers, she lost the clearness and simplicity of vision, which would have enabled her to discern the purposes for which she should employ her strength. Her aims ceased to be wholly Christian. They became in great measure political; and in truth the mediæval history of the Church is the record of the contest between the spiritual and political influences within her, and of the inconsistencies which resulted from an anomalous and amphibious portion. At times, as in the Merovingian period in Gaul, or in the tenth and early part of the eleventh centuries, the religious character seems almost lost, till it is reasserted, as in the time of Louis le Debonair, or of Hildebrand, by a revival whose narrow ecclesiastical character indicates reaction from a secularized system. In this twofold character of the Mediæval Church, of which the warrior bishop and the monk bishop represent each a side, we recognize the explanation of its ambiguous attitude towards slavery. The Church, because it represented Christianity, combated serfdom, at least in its abuses: it becomes itself a serf-holding power, because it had identified itself with the existing political system, and the dominant political class. It encouraged emancipation, yet it held serfs whom it had no intention to emancipate. Recognizing the paradox, we see that the Christianity which encountered serfdom was not of a kind to employ Christian principles, without considerable reserve, or careful accommodation to the political conditions to whose maintenance the Church was so deeply pledged.

The action of the Mediæval Church upon serfdom falls then naturally under two heads: 1. its action as a political and serf-holding power, 2. its action as a spiritual power, outside the political system, and claiming over it rights of surveillance and correction.

22222222222

1. The Church held serfs as early and as late in mediæval history as the secular proprietors. "The devout," says Gibbon[c], "crowded to shelter themselves around the shrine of a popular saint," as "under the battlements of a powerful chief: their submission was accepted by these temporal and spiritual patrons, and the hasty transaction irrevocably fixed their own condition and that of their latest posterity." Thus ecclesiastical and lay serfdom began together; and the earliest testimony to the kind influence of the Church in this its more political form, is the eagerness with which those upon whom hard times were forcing serfdom of some kind preferred ecclesiastical to lay masters.

The possession of serfs by the Church, whatever may be thought of it in principle, found a justification in two great benefits which it conferred on that class. First, it offered to a very large number of them, large in proportion to the vast extent of the Church lands, a service far more tolerable than that of the lay masters. But, secondly, this gentler rule was a standing example and pattern for other proprietors.

We must prove this superiority in the condition and treatment of the ecclesiastical slaves.

α. From them the clergy were drawn: thus they enjoyed the privilege of hope. They could look forward to something better than their present position. It is true that the position of the lower clergy had lost in dignity; that the secular relation of lord and serf was apt to reproduce itself under an ecclesiastical shape in that of the prince, bishop, and the low-born parish priest: that we must not neglect such evidence as that of the 119th Canon of the Council of Aachen[d], held in 817, which enjoins the Bishops to refrain from their habit of ordaining the lower clergy from among the serfs of the Church, with a view to enforce their submission to ecclesiastics by the stripes to which as serfs they were liable. All this is true, and it is only one instance of

[c] Chap. XXXVIII.   [d] Harduin, iv. 1133 A.

the way in which the intrusion of secular ideas and prejudices interfered with the operation of Christian principles.
Yet the most despised priest was in a condition at least less
mean than that of the serf; and, doubtless, at all times he
had some chance of promotion, if he had the ability or piety
to deserve it. The importance of individual ecclesiastics,
unquestionably low-born, is a proof of this : there is other
evidence, in the complaint of Thegan quoted above, " that
the highest offices in the Church were filled by persons the
vilest."

This chance of rising to a high place as an ecclesiastic
was a hope of distinction, and the only one, which was
more or less available to the serfs generally : but it specially
belonged to the ecclesiastical serfs, because a greater care
for their education had rendered them more fit for it, and
there was no obstacle, such as the reluctance of masters,
constituted in other cases. For the Church carefully re-
spected the rights of property, would allow no ordination
of serfs without their master's leave ; condemned to a twofold penalty the ordaining Bishop [e], or cancelled the orders
which he had conferred [f]. In this the Mediæval Church
only followed the law of Valentinian, and the rule of Leo
the Great in the ancient period. Proofs are not cited on
account of their abundance. The regulation is constantly
repeated by the Councils—a repetition from which it is
natural to infer that in this respect the serfs often obtained
advantage from an illicit relaxation of the rule.

β. The Church recognized a higher responsibility towards its serfs. The clergy were not allowed to regard
them merely as property ; they were not to be sold [g]. The
Council of Merida in 666 checked the arbitrary power of

[e] Conc. Aurel. Hard. ii. 1010 ; repeated, Conc. Worms, 868, Can. 40. Hard.
v. 743.
[f] Council of Aachen, 817.
[g] Council of Soissons, Hard. v. 55 E.

individual ecclesiastics over their serfs, prescribed light and decent punishments, and gave the Bishop the sole authority to punish. The 11th Council of Toledo (675) gives the reason for a similar prohibition, when it forbids such punishments inflicted "his a quibus Domini sacramenta tractanda sunt." In the monastic and cathedral schools they were provided with education : this was, as has been seen, a reason for their promotion to Holy Orders.

γ. The Church may have neglected, no doubt it did often neglect, its own responsibilities and duties towards its serfs; but it did not forget to defend them against others. The meanest ecclesiastical serf was safe under the guarantee which secured everything that belonged to Holy Church. His master's charity might sleep : not so the vigilance with which the Church guarded against any breach, however small, of her privileges and immunities. There is a curious letter of Pope Paschal II.,[b] written in 1114, which at once exhibits this vigilance, and shews what were the secular privileges which the Church claimed for its serfs. It was a mistake, we find, to confound them with other serfs by applying to them the same name, "Ecclesiæ famuli, qui apud vos (he is writing to the Bishop and Chapter of Paris) servi vulgo *improprie* nuncupantur." And this verbal confusion had been the sign of an actual abuse ; the evidence of these ecclesiastical "domestics" against freemen had been rejected in judicial proceedings : this was to treat them as if they were common serfs, and to violate a privilege which was as old as the era of the Ripuarian Laws[i]. Paschal prohibits, as King Louis VI. had already done, this innovation, "neque enim æquum est ecclesiasticam *familiam* usdem conditionibus coërceri quibus *servi* sæcularum hominum." In the Synod of 744, the "servi clericales" are allowed the same privilege as the "clerici" themselves:

b Ep. LXII. quoted by Harduin, vol. vi. pt. II. 1819 E.
i Baluze, i. 13. Rip. Law, LVIII. xx.

they are exempted from the vexation of "judices et actores publici."

δ. The serfs of the Church were doubtless exposed to fewer exactions, owing to the character of their masters. Making all allowance for exceptions in the shape of fighting bishops and political ecclesiastics, the ecclesiastical lords stood more aloof than the lay from war and its expenses : there were fewer cases in which contributions had to be levied for their ransom : their serfs were less often called out to serve in war, and were less liable to the incursions of an exasperated enemy, or the exactions of an impoverished master.

These seem to be some of the definite advantages which raised ecclesiastical serfs to a position of superiority over their fellows. That in some way they were superior would be proved by the mere fact of the eagerness with which the serfs of others seized the opportunity of passing into the hands of the clergy[j]. The increase of the Church lands distributed the boon more widely, while all danger of its withdrawal was removed by the rule which prohibited all alienation of Church property, making, in the case of the serf, the single significant exception that ecclesiastics can part with their serfs in favour of liberty alone[k].

2. It is time to pass to the influence exercised upon serfdom generally by the Church, as a spiritual power enforcing Christian principles upon the proprietors. It is best at once to admit that as it has been already allowed that Christianity could not abolish slavery, so it must be allowed that it failed to remove many of its harsher features. The absolute rights of the lord over the body and property of the slave, the violation of his family ties, the distinction as to satisfaction (wehrgeld) and punishments (the slave would

---

[j] Motley's Dutch Republic, i. 32. Even freemen seem to have preferred sometimes ecclesiastical serfdom. Baluze, t. i. col. 725.

[k] Councils of Agde 506, Orleans 541, Soissons 853.

be beaten, where the free man was fined[1]), the rejection of his evidence in law courts, all these remained. Yet the clergy were not powerless to mitigate, whether by laws issued at their instigation, or by their own ecclesiastical canons, or by their influence over individuals, the hardships of the lowest class. It was easier to modify the laws than it had been in Imperial days, because there was no systematic and logical jurisprudence which repelled change; and it was easier to command society and opinion, at least in a superficial way, because all were now in name Christians; and almost all in some degree, or at some moments, amenable to the terrors and promises of the Church. On the other hand, it is of most importance to notice, and it may be done at this opportunity, that this universality of a nominal Christianity destroyed the *esprit de corps* which had existed among Christians, most powerfully while they were an isolated and despised body, but to some degree so long as there were pagans from whom to distinguish them, and which served greatly to make men realize the doctrines of brotherhood taught by Christianity. That which is universal is apt to be unobserved : it is contrast that awakens attention.

The title " defenders of slaves," which was sometimes given to the Mediæval Clergy, inaugurates well this part of the subject.

α. The Church defended them against ill usage. Legally the masters had absolute power, but the Church interposed to check its exercise by her authority over conscience. The privileges of " sanctuary " were the means by which this became an effectual control. The slaves took refuge in the precinct : and the Church, though it recognized the obligation to return them, assumed the right of imposing conditions. For this there were precedents in Roman history. The pagan shrine had secured something to its suppliant

[1] Council of Berkhampstead, Cann. xi. xii. Hard. HI. 1819.

after the rescript of Antoninus: and in regard to Christian sanctuaries it had been provided that the clergy should intercede with the master before returning the slave. Among the new nation, it became the custom to exact a definite oath of amnesty from the masters. There is no rule about slavery so often repeated as this. One example will suffice : that of the Council of Orleans, held in 549, by whose 22nd Canon [m] this oath is exacted, and a pagan master is required to find Christian security for its observance [n]. Besides this sacred shelter, the Church interfered directly by penal regulations to prevent ill-treatment of the serf. Imitating the law of the Empire, the Council of Epaone, in the sixth century, forbade in a Canon, repeated at Toledo in 694, at Worms in 868 [o], the execution of a slave by his master without the magistrate's authority. From the old Jewish Law the capitularies of Charlemagne borrowed *verbatim* the provisions which gave freedom to the slave who lost his eye by his master's violence, and punished the master whose ill-treatment caused his slave's immediate death [p]. It is worthy of note that this Carolingian legislation, in which ecclesiastics had so great a share, abounds in provisions in favour of the slaves; such, for instance, as the mitigation of the fugitive slave laws [q]. Similarly, the Council of Worms repeals a Canon of Illiberis (305), inflicting heavy penalties on the mistress who caused the death of her attendant (ancilla) by beating. In an early English regulation the character of the penalty betrays its source: the master who kills or wounds his slave is punished by a three years' fast. Sad revelations these of a state of

[m] Hard. II. 1447.

[n] Some interesting examples of the flight of slaves to sanctuary in Anglo-Saxon England are quoted, but without authorities, by Wright, Hist. of Domestic Manners and Sentiments, p. 56.

[o] Capitularies, Add. IV. 49. Baluze.

[p] vi. 11 and 14. ed. Baluze.

[q] Baluze, vol. 1. passim. Hallam's Mid. Ages, I. 198, n.

society where such regulations were needed; yet testifying to the incessant beneficence of the Christian Church.

β. However small the family rights of the serfs, there was a point at which the Church undertook their defence. It is time that the codes of the new nations fully adopted the never conquered prejudice of the Roman Law against the intermarriage of slave and free[r], so that our own learned Abp. Theodore lays down[s], that the free shall marry with the free; and that in the laws of France and many nations of Europe, though not of our own, the free man who married a slave woman became himself a slave[t], the Mediæval law herein outdoing the Roman, since Alexander Severus had secured the man's freedom in such a case[u]: that the Church withdrew from the convicted slave rights of marriage which she had herself conferred, as she recalled for a similar reason her ordination gifts[x]; allowing a man or woman married as free, to be discarded if the freedom was afterwards disproved. But in the same period, the time of the Carolinguians, to which the two last mentioned rules belong, it is enacted in the capitularies[y], that the marriage of slaves, to which masters have once consented, cannot afterwards be annulled. This is done with an appeal to the religious principle, "What God hath joined together, let not man put asunder." The serfs then are capable of legitimate marriage, only such marriages must not be made in a way which would defeat the lord's rights.

γ. Misery is not complete till hope is lost: and the mediæval serf owed to the Church his hopes of freedom. Nor were these hopes shadowy. For the Church consistently extolled and enjoined the practice of manumission: it was one of the acts of charity which she steadily taught, and which,

[r] Salic and Visigothic Laws, Ducange, Art. Servi.
[s] Capitula XVII.　　　[t] Ducange, vi. 222.
[u] C. J. vii. XVI. 3.　　　[x] Conc. Wormat. 742.
[y] Baluze, t. I. Col. 1166, &c.

especially, she recommended in opportunities, when those wild fits of panic-stricken remorse, which in an age of half-tamed and uncontrollable characters alternated constantly with the reckless excesses of unbridled crime, secured obedience. The Mortmain Statutes remain to prove how great was the effect of recommendation offered at such times. Men grasped eagerly at the works of charity, which might, as they hoped, cover the multitude of sins: and among these works the sacrifice of property by the donation of freedom was conspicuous. It is mentioned as the practice of the kings of the Franks, that at the birth of a son they emancipated three slaves on each of their domain: the Church watched for the joy of the day of festivity, as she did for the agony of death-bed penitence, and turned them both to the same account. It is said, that in France a pretty custom long lingered to preserve the memory of the manumissions which had so fitly celebrated the great festivals in earlier times: when there was no longer human captivity to relieve, they would open the dove-cotes on the great days and let the birds go free[z].

The preambles of the charters of manumission best prove their Christian origin, as when one says that he does this for the safety of his soul[a]: or another, that he frees his slaves and obeys the commandment, "Be not ye called masters," in order that God may release him from his own sins. "We give and grant A.B.," says a third, "to the Lord God, and the Blessed Virgin, and all the saints[b]." In their control over the courts of law the clergy could and did favour emancipation by turning the scale, as their Roman predecessors had done before them, in favour of liberty in doubtful cases[c].

But the times were lawless. The manumitted slave had

---

[z] Ozanam Civ. du 5me Siècle, ii. 57.
[a] Marculfi Formulæ, II. 32—34. Script. rer. Gall. IV. 498, 499.
[b] Ducange, vi. 223.   [c] Littleton, 205, 6.

much to fear for his newly-acquired freedom. The Church came to his rescue. Here she was sure of her ground. She was on the side of the law. Accordingly she acted vigorously, renewing over and over again her anathemas against the robbers of liberty, and intrusting the execution of these edicts to her clergy, the only organized and vigilant police in the middle age. Certain classes of freedom had a special right to this defence. Some had been manumitted in the Church or within its precinct. Some had commended themselves or been commended to its protection. In making a charter of freedom a master would often add, with an almost whimsical distrust of his own intentions and a wholesome uncertainty as to those of his successors, a clause invoking spiritual penalties upon himself or any of his posterity who should try to withdraw the gift of freedom. There was often a clause in testaments which specially commended those emancipated under them to the protection of the Church—another proof by the way as to the quarter from which the influences favourable to emancipation came. All these the Church lay under special obligation to protect. But in the seventh canon of Macon (585) this protection is extended to other freedmen who had no such special claim to it, and we learn how much it was needed: the secular judges were partial; and, as a remedy, the council enacted that to bishops alone, or to others with their leave, the cognizance of cases of status should belong[d].

δ. As Christianity, on the one hand, helped slaves to become free, so, on the other, she defended freemen from the danger of becoming slaves. Against the slave trade, as carried on with unbelievers, she steadily set her face. Her prohibitions were frequent and peremptory[e], and seem to have been supported by public opinion. The sentiment of

[d] v. to same effect, Conc. Agd. 506. Can. 29.

[e] Conc. Lept. 743,4; Macon. 581, Can. 6; Toledo, 589. Can. 14; Ænhiam, 1009; Lanfranc and Wulfstan, in Gul. Malmesb. p. 302, (ed. Bohn); Laws of Frederick II.

the brotherhood, which unites all Christians in a unity deeper than all external differences, started into life at the contact of Jew and Saracen, and in the new phrase " Christendom," found an appropriate symbol and expression. The sentiment of exclusiveness, natural to an aristocratic society, made this feeling something too defiant to those outside the pale : but, inside, it did nothing but good, and anything which stimulated it served the cause of humanity and civilization. Venice, one of the few places where the trade was common, was, of all European cities, the one least influenced by the Church. But, even within Christendom, the trade was not unopposed. Next to the trade with unbelievers, the sale of men outside their own country seems to have been considered its worst form. In the seventh century, this is forbidden by the Frank queen, Bathildis; and the Council of London, in 1102[f], denounced the extensive commerce by which English slaves were poured into Ireland. The Council of Coblenz, also, in 922[g], forbade the slave trade in general terms. A tale is told of a saint who meets one whom formerly he had sold into slavery. He prostrates himself in penitence before his injured servant, and insists on receiving public punishment at his hands[h].

The real importance of these acts of abolition is due to the fact that they forwarded the disappearance of pure slavery from the Western Countries. It is impossible not to allude to this distinction between slaves and serfs, though, in what has been said, the laws and actions regarding them have been treated indiscriminately. This treatment is, probably, justified by the difficulty of finding out in each case to which class the obscure and not precise language of mediæval documents intends to refer; and by the fact that

[f] Can. 27. (Wilkins I. 383.) "it hath hitherto been the common custom of England."
[g] Can. 7.　　　　　　　　　[h] Acta Sanct. Ord. S. Benedicti II. 400.

the Church acted much in the same way towards both, and that they were really, in many ways, in the same condition. The serf had a home of his own, and even lands of his own; and though these were absolutely at his master's disposal, yet even so precarious an independence raised him morally above the domestic slave, or the agricultural gang-slave of the Empire, stalled and fed, like the animal, in his master's house, and at his expense. If the serf's comforts were perhaps fewer, yet the responsibilities of a home and its maintenance raised him higher in the scale of humanity; and his connection with the soil, from which, usually, he was inseparable, gave scope for the humanizing influence of local and family attachments. Otherwise he would seem to have been in most essential respects as destitute of rights as the slave. That the two classes were quite distinct, is, however, proved by direct statements. The Anglo-Saxon Theowes, for instance, were very different from the Ceorls, who afterwards sank into serfdom; and the slaves whom the Franks, like the other Teutonic nations described by Tacitus, possessed and brought into Gaul, were distinct from the mass of the peasantry, whose condition rapidly became that known as serfdom, or villeinage.

Slavery proper seems to have been uncommon after the eleventh century; in England, the Norman conquest was an important stage in its downfall, since the villeinage, which under them became more general, elevated the theowe as much as it depressed the ceorl. Now, although the substitution of serfdom for slavery is another case of a change due rather to alterations in the general condition of society than to any single cause, yet the Church may claim the credit of having helped it. The attacks upon the slave-trade struck at its supplies; and the contempt for labour, which would have sunk the serf to the level of the slave, was mitigated by the teaching of Christianity, and the eminent example of the monks. In a word, it was probably Christianity which prevented the distinction between freeman and villein from being a caste distinction—it was very nearly this, but not quite—and in the end thus made all the difference: the dividing barrier was one which it was not necessary to overleap or to storm, but which could be silently effaced; and serfdom passed imperceptibly into freedom, without the need of a sweeping measure, changing at once the condition of the whole class, such as tradition, interest, and prejudice would have made it hard or impossible to carry. There are other smaller matters: the *peculium* guaranteed to the slave, at least for the purchase of his liberty[i], or given him upon emancipation[k], the Sunday's rest, for which the Council of Berkhampstead stipulated[l], are instances of boons which might easily be multiplied beyond the limits now possible. In a thousand ways the serf was better off by reason of the Church's help. If neither her Services nor her sacred buildings presented so vividly, as in primitive times, the spectacle of equality before God, if in her doctrinal teaching about the Eucharist, and in the method of celebration, its character as an act of Communion between Christian brethren, was less regarded and less impressed upon the congregation than its sacrificial or sacramental qualities, yet the gorgeous ceremonial, the magnificent architecture of cathedral and abbey, or the quiet repose and simple exhortations of the parish Church, in which he approached God, and received divine gifts, could not but elevate and console the serf. The dignity of the human soul was preserved; and the serf was acquainted with that which gave to life, however wretched, its value and interest. On the other hand, the masters too listened to the Church's voice. They heard the precepts of love and mercy reiter-

[i] Capitula of Theodore, cxvii. Conc. Tolet. 633. Can. 72.
[k] Script. Rer. Gall. vi. 657.
[l] Harduin, III. 1819. A.D. 697.

ated : they could not be ignorant of their duty, though they might ignore it. Some listened and obeyed: to others, the echo of the words came back in other days, when danger or sickness had softened and alarmed their hearts; and even the more reckless and defiant were not so impervious but that the general standard of opinion and practice was raised. If it was the weakness of mediæval Christianity that it was too universal, and therefore too conventional, yet, for that very reason, it influenced more irresistibly the tone of worldly and general society.

In her beneficent action, which dealt to each generation its measure of help and comfort, the Church had no system of distant policy. Yet none the less did she advance unconsciously the brighter future; and, as she awoke the courage and sustained the endurance of the serf, or pleaded with the masters the rights of men, who, if in law their chattels, were in religion their brethren, she smoothed the way for the quicker and more prosperous course of the social revolution, which invested the serfs with the rights and duties of freedom. Unaided, she could not have accomplished, nor was she inclined to attempt, a great act of Emancipation : be it her credit that through the dark and gloomy times, which would have extinguished or wearied any energy less divine, she sowed in silence, uncheered by any ambitious visions, unconscious of the full tendencies of what she did, simply because she strove to fulfil the plain duties of the day, the harvest of the unimagined future.

iii. To the Christian apologist, nothing in the history of slavery is more disheartening, and, to the lover of Christianity, nothing sadder, than to turn from exultation over the fall of mediæval serfdom, and find himself witness to the formation, and to the maintenance through three centuries, in Christian countries and under the eyes of Christian governments, of a slave system entirely new, and, if possible, more complete, odious, and stubborn than any of its predecessors.

In face of this, it might seem useless to talk any more of the power of Christianity against evil. Yet, in the short space left, the endeavour will be made to clear Christianity from this charge ; and to show that, although powerless to prevent the establishment, or, single-handed, to achieve the abolition of slavery, she has yet not wholly neglected her duty, nor failed of success.

In the first place, according to the view maintained throughout this Essay, the Church has not power to defy all other forces, and violently change the course of history : the reason being, that only the few are thoroughly religious, and that the course of the world is mainly decided by other motives (usually those of selfishness and interest), which sway men more generally.

Armed with this assumption, we approach the case of modern slavery, and now see that its foundation was not surprising, since (α) the circumstances were very exceptional ; (β) the selfish and interested motives overpoweringly strong; (γ) and the conditions specially unfavourable to Christian influence.

α. The circumstances were exceptional. In other words, they were quite unlike anything in the old countries: and therefore the substitution of free for slave labour in Europe afforded no precedent. Voluntary labour was not to be had : the division of classes was as strong as it always is when it coincides with the division between conquerors and conquered ; and therefore it might seem that both for the supply of food, and for the maintenance of order, a slave-system was the only resource.

β. If this seemed politically desirable, it also commended itself to every selfish interest. The conquerors were few, and the mines offered them inexhaustible wealth; each individual among them might expect a fortune, if he was

E

allowed to gather this wealth by the employment of slaves, of whom an indefinite supply was secured by the infinite disparity in military skill and equipment, which put the conquered races at the mercy of their victors. These races had themselves enslaved their captives: they could not complain if by a turn of the wheel they shared the fate which they had been accustomed to inflict. They would not work unless compelled: and, if idle, they might be dangerous. Moreover, there was no alternative; the climate made labour impossible to European constitutions, so that the toil of his own hands, while it brought in but small returns, would have exposed the white to almost certain death. The excitement of conquest and adventure disinclined him to a settled and toilsome life: the booty of rich countries made him impatient of the slow profits of industry, and as a conqueror he despised the conquered. Thus avarice, insolence, and pride combined to establish a system which might be plausibly justified even on grounds of prudence.

γ. Lastly, the noise of this wild and turbulent life was no happy sphere for Christian influence. It is curious that in each period of slavery, Christianity has had special difficulties to encounter in the character of the men with whom she has dealt. In Rome she struggled with men exposed to the hardening and corrupting influences of elaborate civilization and extravagant luxury: in the Middle Ages with the wild, untamed natures which had hardly emerged— they had not emerged—from the condition of barbarians. And now again, having known at Rome and Byzantium the special obstacles which the crowd and conventionalities of a metropolis offer to a reformer, she had to deal in the sixteenth century with the wild licentiousness of distant dependencies, which attracted the criminals and desperadoes of every nation under the sun. Evil travels faster than good: and it is only when life and heat are unusually glowing in the heart that its impulse is strong enough fully to supply the extremities. The offscourings of civilization, men who hunted Indians with blood-hounds, as masters, and degraded pagan races as slaves, were unpromising material for Christian energy. It is hardly possible not to see here an instance of the rule, that the worst evil is that which the highest good produces by reaction, or itself becomes. The atrocities of American slavery, perhaps, could hardly have been committed by any but those who, having known the light of Christianity and its ideal of mercy, had wilfully turned away to the works of darkness.

If, in this way, an answer in any degree satisfactory has been given to the difficult question suggested by the existence of American slavery, it only remains to point out what Christianity has done in regard to it, and to credit her with the praises which she rightly deserves. This will be most simply and shortly done by observing how the periods of Christian history coincide with phases in that of slavery. It may be shown that the times of the Church's more active life are those in which slavery was either mitigated or attacked, that the era of darkest iniquity coincided with that of her torpor. Not, of course, that Christianity is guiltless of this lethargy, but only that it is unfair to draw from such a time any inferences as to the power of genuine and active Christianity.

At starting a paradox arises. The sixteenth century, from which the slavery of the negroes dates, was remarkable for a special development of religious life. Never for centuries had there been a time of so much sincerity and zeal: the new communities and the old Church were animated by the same warm rush of fervent life, and kindled it again by their competition into fresh activity. The spread of conquest and discovery seemed for the time hardly to outstrip the activity of the Church; Xavier and the Jesuit missionaries were spreading the Gospel in the farthest East: the New Indies of the West swarmed with the cowls of the Franciscans and Dominicans. It seems that if this was the time at which negro slavery was inaugurated the suggested parallel must be quite delusive. The answer is, that this is the truth, but not the whole truth. Negro slavery was established at that time : but by whom ? and why ? By Christian missionaries, for the defence of a helpless people. The fact that Las Casas was the father of negro slavery, is one of the paradoxes of history : but it can hardly deceive any one for a moment, as to the action of the Christianity which he represented. It was, one may say, a pure accident : and the blame of it falls upon the foresight, and not on the humanity, of the apostle of the Indies. It was a political blunder : not a fault. The real question with which Las Casas had to deal, and by the attitude to which the Christianity of his time must be judged, was the treatment of the conquered races of the New Countries. This was no easy task : the converging force of the causes alluded to above, tended almost irresistibly towards a slave system : and the difficulty of resistance is proved by the acquiescence of a man so fervent and unflinching as Las Casas, in the compromise which saved the red man by enslaving the black. Considering these difficulties, the Christianity of the sixteenth century was not unworthy of its name. It shewed itself in popes and ecclesiastics, in statesmen and commanders. Pius II. had already denounced those who entered the missionary settlements of the Guinea Coast, and reduced the neophytes to slavery; in 1537, Paul III. published a bull against all who should in any wise enslave the Indians of the East or West. Among lower ecclesiastics, Las Casas, whose life was spent in voyages between the two worlds for the prosecution of schemes on behalf of the Indians, or in the attempt to realize some of these schemes by practical experiment, was, although the most eminent, by no means the only champion of the natives; the commission sent out from Spain at Las Casas' instigation was composed of friars; if there were some of the orders who fell into luxury and sloth, yet many assisted Las Casas, or set on foot the missions which have played so much part in South America. They have been bright spots, when all else has been dark: and have shown that the Church could not only declaim against the iniquities of others, but could set an example of another method, by which she did what slave institutions have professed to do, but have never done: she trained the natives into fitness for a higher grade of religion and civilization. In men of the world we find with even more interest, because with greater surprise, proofs of the influence of Christianity. The vigorous policy with which Ximenes entertained and acted upon the representations of Las Casas, his bold demolition of some of the worst features of the system, his frank declaration of the free condition of the Indians, were the acts and words of a cardinal, as well as of a statesman. But his policy was maintained in some degree by his successors. The government annulled the repartimientos which Cortes had granted: it issued commissions which produced voluminous blue books. "It is impossible to peruse them," says one of the few who has done it, "without a deep conviction of the pains taken by the Crown to ascertain the nature of the abuses in the domestic government of the Colonies, and their honest purpose to amend them[m]." "Unfortunately," he adds, "it was found much easier to get this information, than to profit by it[n]." The attempt to do so was made in 1542, at the instigation of the indefatigable Dominican, by the publication of a code: a certain date was fixed at which all slavery was to be abolished: compulsory labour under the repartimiento system, now recognized as a necessity, was limited in amount. Turning from the home governments to the

[m] Prescott, Peru, ii. 228, n.   [n] Prescott, Peru, ii. 231.

officers whom they sent out, the great Gasca, Viceroy of Peru, himself an ecclesiastic, and once a member of the Council of the Inquisition, is an eminent example of a Christian ruler°. Entrusted with the task of re-settling Peru, he published regulations very similar to those just mentioned. His beneficence was attested by the voluntary testimonial which the Indians pressed upon him at his departure. And here, at least, the good was more than temporary: the Government steadily persevered in its charitable designs, and no discontent among subjects has ever been more creditable to the Government than that which was excited among the Peruvian Spaniards " by the constancy of the Audience in enforcing the benevolent restrictions as to the personal services of the natives." Thus the humane policy of the Spanish Government was no temporary result of the gentle and pious disposition of Isabella, but was maintained by Charles V., and bore, perhaps, its best fruits in the stern reign of Philip II. Even among the adventurers who led the conquests, we have an eminent example of the authority of Christian principles. Cortes had, as has been said, sanctioned the principle of repartimientos, which the Government afterwards fruitlessly annulled: but he witnessed by the professions of reluctance[p] with which he accompanied his sanction to the religious feeling of the time, and he gave it practical effect in the regulations[q] by which he strove to prevent the worst abuses of the system. One of these rules, charging the master with the duty of supplying religious instruction to his Indians, proves, like his successful appeal to the Home Government for a body of pious and earnest clergy to convert the Mexicans, the character of the motives which actuated him.

The difficulty with regard to the sixteenth century is,

° Prescott, Peru, ii. 414.   [p] Prescott, Mexico, iii. 232, 3.
[q] Prescott, Mexico, iii. 233.

therefore, one which vanishes on examination. The great feature of the time was the conquest of the great countries of the new world : the great problem how to deal with their inhabitants. The colonists, as might have been expected from their character, tried to give that problem the solution which passion and avarice suggested ; but Christian governments, and the representatives of the Church, addressed themselves to it in a manner not unworthy of Christianity. If, while so absorbed, they allowed another evil, of which it was impossible to foresee the future proportions to creep in, this can hardly be a matter of surprise, still less of blame. The government of Ximenes or of Gasca would have known how to deal with negro slavery in its turn, had that come up for settlement during their tenure of power. And though unfortunately the spirit which had inspired them did not live in their successors, still, while yet the sixteenth century continued, the strength of the prejudice against slavery in Christian Europe is avouched by the history of the beginnings of the slave trade. Montesquieu says[r], that Louis XIII. of France, when he made his edict, which provided that all Africans coming into his colonies should be made slaves, was only reconciled to the step by the argument that this method opened the best prospect of their conversion; an argument which had already imposed on Ferdinand and Isabella, and which had to be urged upon the wretched Louis XV. before even he could be induced to tamper with the principle that slaves landing in France should be made free. Queen Elizabeth, when she heard of the beginning of the slave trade by Hawkins, raised her protest against it.

There followed a dark and gloomy time. At home the glow of religious enthusiasm, after being kindled for a time during the seventeenth century into a devouring flame by the fuel of political animosity, had burnt itself out, and a time of deadness, torpor, and conventionality succeeded, in

[r] Esp. des Lois XV. 4.

which infidelity only spread the more certainly and easily, because a superficial veneer of Christianity deceived men into the belief that all was well with religion, as of old. Lethargy and indifference at home were naturally accompanied by inaction abroad. The Church of England permitted cities to spread and population to increase, without rousing herself to consider and meet their spiritual wants: no wonder that the American Church had to go unprovided with an Episcopate, until, despairing of help from England, they turned to seek the consecration of Bishop Seabury from the despised Episcopalians of Scotland. The Christian apologist will not be surprised, he will even in a sense rejoice, to find that in this period there was little energy to remedy or abolish slavery. Unopposed by any active Christian efforts, it developed into a system so atrocious that no plea of exaggeration can possibly palliate it, and so deep-rooted that it has hardly yet given way. Yet we entertain with pleasure one or two reflections upon a period which otherwise we willingly dismiss. The first is, that all through this time the opinion of the Christian world was in theory hostile to slavery: such opinion, for instance, is that which finds expression in literature. Of poets and writers of fiction, Clarkson has quoted Steele, Pope, Thomson, Savage, Shenstone, Cowper, and Sterne; among philosophers, Hutcheson, Montesquieu, Smith, and Paley, as lifting their voice against it. Not that all this came to anything, the protests were worthless so far as action went; but they shew the fibre, so to say, of the ideas congenial to a society bred in the traditions of many centuries of Christianity. The second reflection is, that if the connection between Christian influence and attacks upon slavery is supported by the absence of the latter, during a time when Christianity was singularly sluggish, the proof seems almost complete upon finding that such exceptions as these existed precisely in those quarters in which the flame of true Christianity still burnt most brightly. We have spoken of the missions of the Jesuits and others abroad: if we look to England, the most genuine Christianity is to be found among the Nonconformist bodies, the Quakers, and afterwards the Methodists. Now the Quakers, from the time of their foundation as a society till the abolition, set themselves with increasing steadiness to oppose slavery. Fox, their founder, preached to the planters of the West Indies, exhorted them to be merciful to their slaves and release them in due time; his companion, Edmonson, had addressed the negroes with success, and made a fair beginning in the work of bringing them to religion and civilization, only to bring down his own arrest, and an act forbidding Quakers to take negroes to their religious meetings. This policy, inaugurated by their founders, was maintained by a series of discussions and resolutions on the part of their general assembly in England, which were repeated at intervals during the first three quarters of the eighteenth century. Their phraseology, when they speak of those "redeemed by one Saviour," "made equally with ourselves for immortality," testifies that they drew their charity from its one perennial source. Their brethren in America were not less zealous. From 1688 onwards, they worked their way steadily to a clearer acceptance and bolder enunciation of the necessity of abandoning slavery. Pennsylvania began the protest—it was taken up by other parts; in 1754 they published a general manifesto which takes the golden rule for its principle. Whatever their faults, the Quakers have never failed in dealing trenchantly with society and opinion when these have seemed to them to conflict with religious principle: having accepted the principle, they did not shrink from carrying it out; in 1774 they enacted that any Quaker holding a slave should be excluded from the society, and by 1787 there remained none to whom the sentence would have applied. To the same effect, in regard to the present argu-

ment, are the protests of Wesley expressed in his " Thoughts
on Slavery," and frequently introduced into his sermons:
the denunciations of Whitfield, who had been in the slave
countries, against the cruelties there practised: or, going
back to a somewhat earlier period, the fact that Massa-
chusetts, in its origin the most religious of the American
colonies, and in all its history and institutions bearing witness to its origin, was the first of all the States to raise her
voice against slavery. As early as 1645 its general court
rescued a negro who had been " fraudulently and injuri-
ously brought from Guinea[s]," and returned him to his
native country; in 1701 the representatives of Boston were
requested to promote action with a view to 'putting a period
to negro slavery[t],' and in 1712 it was forbidden in a law,
which seems nevertheless to have required repetition in a
more complete form in 1788[u].

Thus in secular opinion however listless, and in active
though isolated religious efforts, the elements of a greater
movement already existed. The century did not close
before the day of awakening came. The noise and horrors
of the French Revolution must not blind us to the character of the general movement, of which that was but one
and the most lamentable of the effects. In truth, in the
last quarter of the eighteenth century, it seemed that the
evil brought its own remedy; society woke in indignation
against itself, it rose in rebellion against its own lethargy:
and the movement of enthusiasm for reform which seized
the upper and ruling classes in France, in the ten years
preceding the Revolution, would have won a larger share of
the attention of history if it had not come too late: the
voice of thunder, in which the lower people spoke their
protest against society, drowned the candid self-accusations
by which society was eagerly exposing its own defects.

[s] Holmes, Ann. of America, i. 278.   [t] Id. ib. 481.
[u] Id. ii. 368.

The greatness of this convulsion, that which, however long history may last, will make it yield to none in interest and importance, lay in its universality. Thus, although it truly brought with it a violent outburst of infidelity, it seemed that religion roused itself in presence of the danger. Aggressive and violent unbelief was met by a more vigorous assertion of Christian faith. These considerations render the great crisis, which took place coincidently in the history of slavery, more intelligible. The year 1787 has already been mentioned, but it was marked by more than one event. Two years before the outbreak of the Revolution it bears evidence of the great upheaving. In that year the Pennsylvanian Abolition Association, containing Quakers and others, was extended and made general ; while, on this side of the water, the little Quaker Society, formed in 1784, was expanded under the auspices of Wilberforce into a general association of all interested in the subject.

It is unnecessary to pursue the steps which ended in the abolition of the trade and the Acts of Emancipation, or to dwell on the motives to which those acts were due. Undoubtedly, an increased zeal for political liberty roused a righteous indignation against a gigantic system of odious tyranny. But, on the one hand, ancient history, proving that this affection for liberty may well coexist with a slave system, enforces the belief that the more comprehensive and philanthropic character of its modern form is the outcome of a society saturated more deeply than it will acknowledge by Christian influence : and, on the other hand, the records of Wilberforce and his friends (to which public attention has recently been again called) show that where it is possible most definitely and directly to trace the motives which brought about the change, they prove to be those of the simplest and purest Christianity. The apologists of slavery have sneered at the sight of a great nation abolishing, amid lofty religious professions, an institution which every sound argument of cool reason would defend, and which it was no sacrifice to them to abandon. Grant that every argument would defend it, that the nation was misled by its conscience, still the glory of the act, as a public acknowledgement of the claim of duty in the sphere of politics, remains as certainly as the successful resistance of interests for twenty years vindicates its self-denying character.

A word remains to be said on the defences set up for slavery within recent times. They bear testimony to Christianity in more ways than one. The pleas which satisfied Louis XIII. and Isabella have been repeated, and the slave trade has been defended for its missionary [w], slave institutions for their educational value. Or, the Bible has been ransacked for arguments; and not only has Noah's curse been made a ground for the perpetual degradation of the negro race, but St. Paul has been quoted on behalf of the fugitive slave laws. Because (as has here been shown) Christianity was not revolutionary, therefore every existing institution, however iniquitous, has claimed the right to dress itself in the livery of her protection. The value of these pleas has not been discussed here; that has been done too recently and too well. They might have weight, if urged to shew that a hasty or sweeping measure, if for other reasons undesirable or dangerous, is not imposed by any intemperate dogmatism on the part of Christianity: urged, as they commonly are, in defence of the indefinite perpetuation of a system like that of the American slave states, they must be ascribed either to gross hypocrisy or gross self-deception. But they exhibit irrefragable proofs of the force of Christian influence. A party never testifies to the power of its adversaries so clearly as when it begins to take their principles, and to attempt by paradoxical inferences to turn them into the grounds of its own defence.

[w] v. Granier de Cassagnac. v. aux Antilles, ii. 480.

These men pay homage in another way when they find it necessary, in making use of Aristotle's old doctrine that slavery is justified by the existence of certain races naturally slave, to seek a proof of this from the evidence of anatomy, ethnology, and other sciences. Christianity has planted the notion of the unity and brotherhood of men so deep, that these philosophers have much to do before they can eradicate it.

Public opinion is now, on the whole, hostile to slavery; yet there are not wanting indications that the reaction from the enthusiasm for liberty, in the direction of despotism, has been accompanied by a tendency to regard the opposition to slavery as sentimental, and to rehabilitate the old theory that these races require the beneficent care of owners to lead them by gentle compulsion to higher things[x]. It is impossible to foresee how much this opinion may gain ground: to be sure that there will be no failure in the active charity which has in so great degree already triumphed over slavery, nor a reaction of public sentiment in its favour. If this should prove to be the case, the great abolition movement of the first half of the nineteenth century would only be another instance of that which seems to be the moral of the whole history—that the influence of the Church over the world at large is only at exceptional moments strong enough to produce great results, and is always liable to turn out more specious than real. Perhaps enemies and friends have alike missed the guidance which the declaration, " that many are called but few chosen," affords in the study of Ecclesiastical History. It is vain to suppose that Christianity can exercise her influence upon the world, except through the disciples who are in heart and will wholly hers; vain to dream that while these are, as they must be, few, she can sway the world

[x] Pall Mall Gazette, March 13, 1869.

or shape its course. Any success over the mass of mankind is a matter for joy; but such success is not to be generally expected, nor its absence regarded as an evidence of failure.

www.ingramcontent.com/pod-product-compliance
Lightning Source LLC
Chambersburg PA
CBHW022141090426
42742CB00010B/1340

* 9 7 8 3 7 4 4 7 3 4 5 0 9 *